name your
PET!

name your
PET!

Dr Rob Miller B. Vet. Sc.

NEW
HOLLAND

First published in Australia in 1998 by New Holland
Publishers (Australia) Pty Ltd
Sydney • Auckland • London • Cape Town

14 Aquatic Drive Frenchs Forest NSW 2086 Australia
1A, 218 Lake Road Northcote Auckland New Zealand
24 Nutford Place London W1H 6DQ United Kingdom
80 McKenzie Street Cape Town 8001 South Africa
Copyright © Dr Rob Miller B.Vet.Sc.

Editor: Maggie Sanders
Designer: Jaffa McCallum
Illustrator: Cheddar Manning
Printer: The Guernsey Press Co. Ltd

National Library of Australia Cataloguing-in-Publication Data:

Miller, Rob.
Name your pet!: over 3500 names.

ISBN 1 86436 431 9

1. Pets - Names. I. Title.

929.97

Cover: Main picture: Felix Rennex; (left to right): Billy
Seibokas, Felix Rennex, Myrtle Seibokas; Title Page: Felix
Rennex; Back Cover: Felix Rennex

Dedicated to Cora and Hannah

Acknowledgements
Many thanks to the clients of Seaforth Veterinary
Hospital for their creativeness (or otherwise!) in
choosing pet names. My thanks to Terry Collins and
Anita Brown for their assistance in compiling the
New Zealand panel of names.

CONTENTS

In The Beginning 8

Disclaimer and Other Facts 9

How to Use This Book 11

1: Names A–Z 12

    Dogs 13

    Cats 32

    Birds 54

    Rabbits 57

    Guinea Pigs 59

2: The Top 100 60

    The Dog Top 100 61

    The Cat Top 100 62

    The Bird Top 40 63

    The Rabbit Top 40 63

    The Guinea Pig Top 40 . . .64

3: Names By Breed 65

    Dogs 66

    Cats 114

4: Names By Themes 145

Australiana 146

Religious Origin 146

Character Names 147

Colour Related 148

Cutie 149

Elegant 149

Famous People 150

Food & Drink 151

Hi Tech 151

Historic 152

Makes Me Laugh! 152

Nature Related 153

New Zealander 154

Original Ideas 155

Place Names 155

Pop Music 156

Potentially Cheeky 156

Pretty 157

5: Summary and Notes on Your Own Pet's name 158

Scoreboard 159

IN THE BEGINNING

When a new baby is on the horizon the household works themselves into a frenzy with baby naming sessions.

The other night I was exposed to this tradition in a four-hour marathon session, suggesting names for my upcoming niece. Madness reigned, my Dad got grumpy (he was trying to watch a movie at the time). He was constantly interrupted by madcap name suggestions and laughter. Admittedly I was in my usual mood of thinking up the most ridiculous names (that's the best part!). In the end my sister wisely ignored me. After exhausting my memory banks she declared, 'I just can't think of what to call it!'

Thus having been snubbed, the prospect of coming up with further suggestions just one day later shook me with dread. I began to think about baby naming books as an alternative. It then struck me that I have never seen the equivalent for pets. Indeed people's suggestions often run riot when it comes to pet naming. After all pets will never complain even if you call them Hercules (try that with your son! He may disagree, especially when a teenager!)

Thus I began my project — Name Your Pet! was born. This did not mean I was about to sit down and subject myself to months of self-inflicted agony. Oh no, I would be far more scientific than that! After all why use my brain when I could pick the brains of thousands of clients, as it were. I have at my disposal the distillate of seven years of family naming sessions with all the torment that goes with that!

Now, if you are still with me at this point I will continue with the family saga. . .

Coming into the home straight my sister had still not chosen a name for her new baby. Things were getting desperate and I had not quite got around to buying her that damned naming book. At this stage she was short listing names and taking a democratic vote (democracy is a mainstay of our family). She rattled off the proposed names — they sounded eerily familiar! Yes she had decided this very book was up to the job, and so the name Hannah was chosen from its pages. From this I conclude that if this book is good enough for my sister then it better be good enough for you, so no complaints!

Disclaimer and Other Facts

I disclaim and deny everything! Why, I'm not sure but it seems prudent to do so.

*This book has no claim to being 'complete' and may not contain every last breed, but it covers most.

*Don't blame me for name misspellings, this is how our clients wanted them spelt!

*I have not edited out any naughty names! The people of this area are very proper and moral and are to be commended.

*The number of names appearing under any breed is proportional (well in a way) to the local popularity of that breed, hence why there are lots of burmese name suggestions while few for the ragdoll.

*Contrary to common belief the names Bonzo or Fido as dog's names ain't popular! What can I say?

• Jessie is the most popular dog's name so don't be boring and call your dog Jessie.

• Misty is the most popular cat's name so don't be boring and call your cat Misty.

• Bird is the most popular Bird's name. Hellfire, surely you can do better than that! So don't call your bird Bird! Bluey at number 2 is a slight improvement.

• Rabbit is the most popular rabbit's name. I'm beginning to see a pattern here. Avoid this name at all costs, otherwise you will hear from me!

• Guinea is the most popular guinea pig's name! How do we explain this scientifically? Well from our above sorrowful points one would expect guinea pig to be the outright winner. However this is a real mouthful (sarcasm here folks), so out of necessity guinea wins out.

• Nick is likely to be the most popular Greek male name, But this is of no consequence to Sydney-siders. Here in Sydney he would likely be called Greek based on the above!

• This last point is to remind you I deny everything. In conclusion, maybe this book will help you name your pet, or maybe it will just give you a good laugh.

How to Use This Book

APPROACH 1:

Isn't it obvious? Just read it, or I'll smash your face in!

APPROACH 2:

For those of you who enjoy the benefit of further direction then note that this book is in four sections.

SECTION 1:

Lists names alphabetically for the species of dog, cat, bird, rabbit, and guinea pig.

SECTION 2:

Top of the pops! We list the most popular 100 dog and cat names in descending order (top 40 for birds, rabbits and guinea pigs).

SECTION 3:

Lists names by species and breed enabling the promulgation of these names within the breed. (For example, for those who want to know a few good old Springer Spaniel names.)

SECTION 4:

Lists names by theme, supposing your pet stimulates a certain feeling as to what it should be called but you can't quite place it.

I hope you find this tome both tomeful and useful, browse on!

NAMES A-Z

DOGS

A

Abbe
Abbey
Abbie
Abby
Aberdeen
Abigail
Abu
Ace
Adage
Adelaide
Adeva
Adolph
Adrian
Affie
Aggie
Agnes
Agro
Ahara
Akeisha
Akela
Ala
Alaska
Albert
Aleutia
Alex
Alexa
Alexander
Alexis
Alf
Alfred
Ali
Alice
Alicia
Allie

Aloysius
Amanda
Amber
Amelia
Ampy
Amy
Andy
Angel
Angus
Anna
Annabelle
Annie
Anzac
Apache
Apollo
Apostrophe
April
Archer
Archibald
Archie
Argus
Ari
Arizona
Arkie
Arko
Arly
Arnie
Arno
Arnold
Arrow
Arthur
Asa
Ashanti
Ashe
Ashlea

Ashley
Assassin
Astro
Astroboy
Athena
Attila
Augustus
Aurora
Aussie
Axel
Axl
Ayla

B

B B
B J
Babes
Babette
Babs
Baby
Bachi
Baci
Badger
Badgie
Badgy
Baffi
Bagel
Bags
Bailey
Bali
Balto
Bam Bam
Bambi
Bandit
Bando

13

NAME YOUR PET!

Banjo
Bankus
Barnes
Barney
Barnie
Barnsy
Baron
Barra
Barrumundi
Bart
Basil
Bass
Baxter
Bayette
Bazil
Bazzie
Bazzle
Bea
Bear
Beasley
Beattie
Beau
Beaubeau
Beaujolais
Beaumont
Becci
Becky
Beebee
Beebes
Beefer
Beetle
Belay
Bella
Belle
Bellejovi
Ben
Benjamin
Benji

Benjy
Bennie
Benny
Benson
Bentleigh
Bentley
Beppu
Bernard
Bernie
Berri
Bert
Bertie
Bess
Bessie
Bessy
Best Pal
Betsy
Betty
Bianca
Biatta
Biddy
Biffy
Big Boy
Biggles
Bikita
Bilbo
Bill
Billie
Billy
Bilson
Bimbo
Bindi
Bindy
Binger
Bingo
Binkie
Binky
Binnie

Binny
Bismark
Black Devil
Black Night
Blackett
Blackie
Blake
Blanche
Blanco
Blast
Blaza
Blaze
Bliss
Blitz
Blocka
Blocker
Blondy
Bloss
Blossom
Blossum
Blue
Blue Nell
Blueberry
Bluey
Bo
Boadicea
Bob
Bobbie
Bobby
Bodie

14

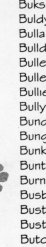

Bodhisattva
Bogart
Bogi
Bollinger
Bolly
Bon Bon
Boner
Boney
Bongo
Bonnie
Bonny
Bonza
Bonzi
Boof
Boofy
Boogie
Boots
Bora
Boris
Bosco
Boshka
Bosley
Boss
Boston
Bosun
Boumba
Bouncer
Bow
Bowie
Bows
Boz
Bozley
Bozo
Brady
Brando
Brandy
Brandy
  Alexander

Braveheart
Brett
Brewster
Bridget
Briggs
Brigitte
Brillow
Brindle
Brodie
Brogie
Bronco
Bronson
Bronte
Brontie
Bronwyn
Brook
Brooke
Brooklyn
Brooky
Bros
Brumby
Bruno
Brut
Bruto
Brutus
Bubba
Bubbalouie
Bubble
Bubbles
Bubush
Buck
Bucky
Bud
Budd
Buddy
Budget
Buffy
Buggs

Buggy
Bugsy
Buksi
Buldy
Bulla
Bulldozer
Bullet
Bullett
Bullie
Bully
Bundy
Bungy
Bunker
Bunty
Burnie
Busby
Busta
Buster
Butch
Buttons
Butts
Buzzy
Byron

C
C D
Caesar
Caleb
Callan
Calvin
Cam
Cameo
Cammie
Cammy
Candy
Cane
Caniche
Cantona

NAME YOUR PET!

Capri	Charlotte	Chrissie
Captain	Charly	Chrissy
Captain Jack	Chato	Christen
Cara	Chauncey	Christie
Carby	Chaz	Chu
Carla	Checker	Chuck
Carly	Chelsea	Chuffie
Carmen	Chelsea	Churchill
Caro	Brown	Chuzz
Cas	Chenoa	Cid
Casey	Cherie	Cider
Cash	Cherran	Ciggi
Casper	Chessie	Cila
Cassandra	Chester	Cinci
Cassegrain	Chet	Cinders
Cassey	Chevy	Cindy
Cassie	Chi	Cissy
Cassy	Chi-Chi	Clancy
Castor	Chicho	Clara
Cathy	Chico	Clare
Cato	Chiko	Clarence
Cedar	Chilli	Claude
Cedric	Chilly	Claudia
Ceiliddh	Chimba	Claudie
Cerberus	China	Clea
Chad	Chinook	Cleo
Chamois	Chip	Cleopatra
Champ	Chipper	Cleveland
Chan	Chippie	Cliff
Chanel	Chips	Clint
Chanti	Chiquita	Cloe
Chao Ren	Chisel	Clover
Char Bon	Chloe	Cluny
Charbon	Choo Choo	Clyde
Charles	Chopin	Coach
Charley	Chou Chou	Cobar
Charlie	Chow	Cobber
Charlie Brown	Choyi	Coco

Coco Chanel
Codee
Codie
Cody
Coke
Collette
Columbus
Comet
Commando
Con
Conan
Connie
Connor
Constanza
Cooee
Coogee
Cooleo
Cooper
Copper
Coquette
Coquin
Coral
Cori
Corky
Cosmo
Cougar
County
Couter
Cracker
Crash
Cruise
Crumpet
Crystal
Cuddles
Cuki
Cully
Cuma
Cupid

Curley
Cyndi
Cyrus

D

D J
Daisy
Daji
Dak
Dallas
Damien
Dan
Dana
Dani
Daniel
Danny
Daphne
Darby
Darth
Dash
Dave
David
Dawn
Dax
Deacon
Debbie
Deco
Deefa
Deisel
Deli
Deputy
Des
Desko
Deva
Devil
Dexter
Dhugal
Di Di

Diamond
Digby
Digger
Dilly
Dimmy
Dimpy
Ding
Dinkie
Dino
Ditto
Diva
Dixie
Dizzy
Djawi
Doba
Dodger
Dodori
Dog
Dolche
Dolly
Dominic
Domino
Donna
Doo Doo
Doods
Doogie
Doolan
Doris
Dorothy
Dorrie
Dotty
Doug
Dougal
Douglas
Dozer
Dr Spock
Dreva
Drummond

NAME YOUR PET!

Duchess
Dude
Dudley
Duff
Dugan
Duke
Dumpster
Duncan
Dusky
Dusty
Dutch
Dutchie
Dylan

E
Ebony
Eccles
Echo
Eddie
Edwina
Ekke
Eleanore
Electra
Elemer
Eli
Elka
Elkie
Ella
Elle
Elley
Ellie
Elliot
Elly
Elmo
Elsa
Else
Elsie
Elvis

Ember
Emi
Emily
Emma
Emmie
Enya
Eppie
Eric
Ernest
Ernie
Eros
Errol
Escher
Eureka
Eva
Evie

F
Fabian
Fang
Fanta
Feather
Fee
Feliny
Felix
Fella
Fergie
Fergus
Fhane
Fifi
Fifty
Figaro
Finn
Fitty
Fizz
Flash
Fletch
Fletcher

Fleur
Flint
Flintstone
Flloyd
Floozy
Floppy
Floss
Flossie
Flossy
Floyd
Flufflett
Fluffy
Flynn
Flyte
Folly
Fonz
Fonzarelli
Fookchai
Footy
Foxie
Foxy
Fran
Frank
Frankie
Franky
Freckles
Fred
Freddy
Frederick
Freebee
Freeway
Freya
Frida
Frieda
Fripon
Fritz
Fritzy
Frodo

Fudge
Fuschia

G
Gabby
Garrick
Gaucho
Geena
Gemini
Gemma
Genie
Geofrey
Geordie
George
Georgi
Georgia
Georgie
Georgie Girl
Gera
Gerry
Gertrude
Gidgit
Gigi
Gila
Gilbert
Gilbey
Gilda
Gilla
Gina
Ginger
Ginny
Gipsy
Girl
Girly
Gizmo
Gladys
Goanna
Godzilla

Gogo
Goldea
Goldie
Goldie Ponx
Goliath
Goloum
Gordon
Gorggy
Gosha
Grace
Greenie
Greta
Gretel
Griff
Grimmy
Grimsley
Grizzly
Groover
Grub
Grumpy
Grungle
Guai
Guinea
Guinness
Gum Nuts
Gunter
Gus
Gussie
Guzzi
Gyp
Gypsy
Gyzmo

H
Hagar
Halley
Hamish
Hamlet

Hannah
Hannibal
Happi
Happy
Harlequin
Harley
Harmony
Harold
Harriet
Harriette
Harrison
Harry
Harvey
Hashish
Hattab
Hattie
Hawk
Heathcliff
Heather
Heathie
Heckle
Hector
Heidi
Hektor
Helga
Helmut
Henderson
Hendrix

Henry
Herbie
Hercules
Herman
Hermie
Hero
Hioni
Hobbs
Hobo
Hoges
Holly
Homer
Honey
Honto
Hooch
Hope
Horatio
Hudson
Huey
Huggy
Hugh
Hugo
Humphrey
Huntly
Hurley
Husha
Hutch
Huxley

I

Iggy
Ike
Ilka
Imogen
Inca
Indi
India
Indiana
Indie
Indigo
Indy
Inky
Iq
Irish
Isaac
Isabel
Isabella
Ishka
Isis
Isobella

J

J D
Jaala
Jack
Jack Daniels
Jacki
Jackie
Jacko
Jackson
Jacob
Jade
Jaegar
Jaffa
Jaga
Jai
Jake
James
Jamey
Jamie
Jamie Lee
Jana
Janey
Jarra
Jashu
Jasmine
Jason
Jaspa
Jasper
Java
Jay
Jay Jay
Jazz
Jazzie
Jazzmine
Jeanne
Jeckle
Jed
Jedda
Jeddah
Jeff
Jefferson
Jemma
Jenken
Jenna
Jenny
Jerry
Jesper
Jess
Jesse
Jessi
Jessica
Jessie
Jessie Belle
Jessief
Jessoe
Jessy
Jester
Jesuis
Jet
Jethro
Jett
Jezabel
Jicky

Jill	**K**	Keeper
Jillaroo	K C	Keesha
Jilly	K T	Kelley
Jim	Kadi	Kellie
Jim Beam	Kahli	Kelly
Jimah	Kahlua	Ken
Jimmy	Kahn	Kenny
Jina	Kai	Kenya
Jinna	Kaiser	Kenza
Jinta	Kaitlin	Kenzie
Jip	Kala	Keppe
Jo	Kali	Kerry
Jo Jo	Kama	Kesh
Jock	Kama-Kazie	Kesha
Jodi	Kane	Kevin
Jodie	Kaos	Khan
Jody	Kara	Kheva
Joe	Karbon	Khia
Joel	Karl	Kiah
Joey	Karla	Kiara
Johnnie	Karma	Kibble
Joli	Karnie	Kiera
Jolly	Kasey	Kiki
Jones	Kashi	Killa
Jonte	Kaspar	Killarney
Jonty	Kasper	Kim
Jordan	Kate	Kimba
Jordie	Katerina	Kimmi
Jordy	Katie	King
Josephine	Kato	King Titus
Josh	Katy	Kinko
Joshua	Kaya	Kip
Josie	Kaydee	Kipper
Judith	Kayla	Kirby
Judy	Kayler	Kiri
Julian	Kazna	Kirra
Junior	Keats	Kirri
Juno	Kee	Kitchener

Kitt
Kiwi
Kiya
Kizzy
Klepsie
Knuckles
Kobi
Kola
Kona
Kong
Kori
Kosie
Kosmo
Kossa
Kostya
Kouki
Koukla
Koyinu
Kristie
Krug
Krusty
Kubilai
Kublai
Kuru
Kushka
Kushla
Ky
Kyah
Kyle
Kysha
Kzar

L
Lace
Lacey
Lachlan
Lad
Laddie
Lady
Lady Effi
Laika
Lance
Landi
Lapsang
Lara
Larrikin
Larry
Lassie
Latte
Laura
Laxy
Layla
Leah
Lecie
Leia
Leisha
Leloy
Lenny
Leo
Leroy
Les
Leslie
Lettie
Levi
Lewis
Lexie
Libby
Lice
Licorice
Liebchen

Lil
Lilie
Lily
Lincoln
Lindy
Lindy Lou
Ling Ling
Link
Lionel
Liquorice
Lisa
Little Boy
Little One
Lizzie
Lizzy
Llasha
Llhana
Lochinvar
Lochley
Lola
Lorenzo
Loretta
Lottie
Lou Lou
Louie
Louis
Louise
Loupo
Luca
Lucia
Lucky
Lucky Dog
Lucy
Lucy Brown
Ludo
Luigi
Luka
Luke

Lulu
Luna
Lupo
Lurar
Lushka
Luther
Lyndy

M
Ma
Mabo
Mac
Macbeth
McCool
McDougal
McDuff
Mack
Mackie
McTavish
Mactavish
Maddi
Maddie
Maddison
Maddy
Made
Madgi
Madii
Madison
Maggie
Maggie May
Magic
Magnum
Magnus
Magpie
Maim
Maisie
Major
Mali

Mambo
Mandy
Mango
Mannie
Manoulis
Manulis
Marcus
Mardi
Mark Twain
Marla
Marlene
Marley
Marlowe
Marquise
Marshall
Martha
Martin
Martine
Marty
Mary
Mask
Matches
Matey
Matic
Matilda
Matrix
Matt
Mattie
Maude
Maverick
Mavis
Max
Maxi
Maxie
Maxine
Maxwell
Maxwell Smart
Mayhem

Mayo
Mbili
Meesha
Meg
Megan
Megs
Megsie
Meka
Melanie
Melodie
Melody
Merlin
Merri
Merry
Mia
Michael
Michelle
Michou
Mick
Micka
Mickey
Mickie
Micky
Micolee
Midge
Midget
Midnight
Miffy
Mikey
Miki
Mikki
Miklmas
Miko
Milamber
Mildred
Millie
Milly
Milo

Milou
Mimi
Mimmy
Mincer
Minder
Mindy
Ming
Mingus
Minky
Minnie
Minny
Minska
Minta
Minte
Minty
Minx
Miranda
Mischa
Mischief
Mish
Misha
Mishka
Misho
Mishy
Missie
Missy
Mister
Misty
Mitch
Mitchell
Mitsi
Mitsy
Mitzi
Mitzy
Miya
Mocha
Moddy
Moet

Mogs
Mogul
Mogus
Mojo
Mollie
Molly
Molson
Monet
Monique
Monoch
Monster
Montague
Monte
Montgomery
Monty
Moo Moo
Moon
Mopsy
Morgan
Moritz
Morrison
Morse
Morticia
Mouse
Moushka
Mozart
Mr Biggles
Mr Fudge
Mr McGoo
Mr Mush
Mr Tuppypuddle
Mudgee
Muffett
Muffin
Muffy
Mufti
Mufty
Muggsy

Munchkin
Mungichi
Mungo
Muppy
Murphy
Murray
Muski
Mustang
Mutley
Myra

N

Nacyre
Nala
Nanaque
Nancy
Nandi
Nanny
Nanuq
Napoleon
Nappa
Narelle
Natasha
Nathaniel
Navarro
Nayia
Ned
Negra
Negus
Nell
Nellie
Nelly
Nelson
Nelson
Nero
Nessie
Newton
Nibbles

Nicholas
Nick
Nicki
Nicky
Niki
Nikita
Nikki
Nimm
Nina
Ninja
Nip
Nipper
Nitro
Noddy
Noni
Nonya
Noodle
Noodles
Nooee
Nosey
Nuff
Nugget
Nushka
Nutmeg

O
O D
O J
O P
Oakleigh
Oberon
Ocker
Oddie
Odessa
Offie
Oggy
O'hara
Oke

Olive
Oliver
Ollie
Olympic
Oocky
Ooshi
Opal
Opit
Orpheus
Orrah
Oscar
Oskar
Otis
Otto
Oz
Ozzie

P
Paddie
Paddington
Paddles
Paddy
Pancho
Panda
Pandy
Pansy
Panza
Panzer
Paris Texas
Patch
Patches
Patchy
Patsy
Paula
Pav
Paw Paw
Pax
Pazazz

Peace
Peaches
Pearl
Pearle
Pebbles
Pedro
Peekay
Peggy
Peggy Sue
Penbeh
Penelope
Penny
Pepa
Pepe
Pepi
Peppa
Pepper
Peppi
Peppie
Peppy
Pepsi
Percy
Perrie
Perrier
Perro
Peta
Petal
Pete
Peter
Petra
Pfeffer
Phantom
Phibi
Philbert
Phoebe
Phoneix
Pibba
Piccolo

NAME YOUR PET!

Pickles
Pie
Pierre
Piglet
Ping
Pinnie
Pip
Pipi
Pippa
Pippi
Pippin
Pippy
Pixie
Pixote
Pluto
Poco
Pogo
Pokie
Pola
Pollux
Polly
Pollyanna
Polo
Polpi
Pom Pom
Pompei
Ponsonby
Ponti
Poochie
Poochy
Pookie
Popcorn
Popeye
Poppet
Poppy
Popsy
Porridge
Portia

Pouncer
Power
Prim
Prince
Princess
Princess
 Pretty
Pripps
Pritzy
Professor
Psyche
Pucci
Puck
Puddie
Puddles
Puddy
Pug
Pugsley
Pugsly
Pugzly
Pumpkin
Pup
Puppy
Purdey
Pym

Q

Quattro
Queensky
Quizzy

R

R 2
Ra
Rachael
Radar
Radcliff
Raff

Raffles
Rafiki
Ragamuffin
Rags
Rahm
Raj
Ralf
Ralph
Ramah
Rambo
Ramses
Rana
Rani
Ransom
Raphael
Raphie
Rasa
Rascal
Rasmus
Rasta
Rastas
Rastus
Ravel
Rayna
Razz
Razzie
Rebel
Red
Reece
Reg
Regan
Reggae
Reggie
Remi
Remington
Remmy
Remo
Remy

Ren
Renegade
Repo
Reuben
Rex
Rexy
Rhea
Rhett
Rhumer
Richmond
Ricky
Ricky Lee
Ridge
Riggins
Rina
Ringo
Ripley
Risk
Risky
River
Robbie
Robbo
Robert
Rocco
Rocket
Rockie
Rocky
Rocky

Rochland
Roger
Rogue
Rohnda
Roisin
Rojo
Roland
Rolf
Rolfe
Roli
Rolly
Roman
Romeo
Rommel
Rommy
Romulus
Ronnie
Rory
Rosa
Rose
Rosey
Rosie
Rosti
Rosy
Roup
Rowdy
Rowf
Rox
Roxanne
Roxi
Roxy
Ruby
Rudi
Rudik
Ruff
Ruffles
Ruffy
Rufus

Rum
Rummy
Runah
Rupert
Ruska
Rusky
Russell
Rustina
Rusty

S
Saas
Saavik
Sabbie
Sabie
Sable
Sabre
Sacha
Sadie
Saffran
Saffy
Safron
Sail
Sake
Sakima
Sally
Sam
Samantha
Samba
Samber
Sambucca
Sammy
Sampson
Samson
Samuel
Samuri
Sanburg
Sandy

27

NAME YOUR PET!

Santa
Sara
Sarah
Sarai
Saravich
Sari
Sascha
Sasha
Sashie
Sasky
Sausage
Saxon
Scaggs
Scally
Scamp
Scampi
Scarlett
Schatze
Schatzie
Schnook
Schultz
Scoobie
Scott
Scottie
Scottie Dog
Scout
Scrappy
Scruff
Scruffie
Scruffles
Scruffy
Scrumpy
Scully
Scuzzie
Sean
Seana
Sebastian
Sebby

Sengay
Seoul
Sequoia
Serge
Sha
Shad
Shadow
Shah
Shaka
Shakespeare
Shampers
Shamrock
Shamus
Shandie
Shandy
Shane
Shaq
Shara
Sharday
Shardii
Shari
Sharkie
Sharky
Sharna
Sharne
Sharni
Shauna
Shay
Shayne
Shaz
Sheba
Shedda
Sheema
Sheena
Shelley
Shelly
Sheltie
Shep

Shergon
Sherman
Sherona
Sherrie
Sherry
Shika
Shimi
Shionach
Shitan
Shona
Shona Mercy
Shoomba
Shoshone
Shoupay
Show Off
Shuftee
Shy
Shyra
Sid
Sidney
Sigmund
  Freud
Silva
Silver
Silvey
Simba
Simpson
Sinbad
Sindy
Sir William
Sirius
Sissy
Siva
Skamp
Skip
Skipper
Skoshi
Sky

Sky Rocket	Southern	Stroka
Skyblue	Sox	Strudel
Skye	Soxy	Stubby
Slam	Spangles	Stud
Sludge	Spanna	Stumpy
Sluggo	Spanner	Sucher
Smarty	Sparky	Suga
Smiggin	Speck	Sugar
Smokey	Specks	Sugsy
Smudge	Spencer	Suie
Snags	Spice	Sukey
Snake	Spider	Suki
Snapper	Spike	Sultan
Snegi	Splash	Summer
Sniffy	Spock	Sumo
Snitch	Sponge	Sundane
Snitzel	Spooky	Sunny
Snooks	Spot	Sunshine
Snoopy	Springer	Sunsie
Snow	Sprocket	Suscha
Snowball	Spud	Sushi
Snowflake	Spunt	Susie
Snowy	Sqizzy	Suske
Snuffles	Squeak	Susy
Snuffy	Stan	Suzie
Snugglepot	Stanzi	Suzy
Socks	Star	Swag
Soda	Steffi	Swampy
Sofie	Stella	Sweep
Sonic	Sting	Sweety
Sonnet	Stiv	Swifty
Sonny	Stoli	Swiggles
Sooki	Stoonce	Sybil
Sooky	Storm	Syd
Sooty	Stormy	Sydney
Sophie	Strauss	Sylvester
Sos	Stregga	Syska
Souchong	Streuth	Systar

NAME YOUR PET!

T

T Bone	Ted	
T C	Teddy	
Tabitha	Teddy Bear	
Tabu	Teemie	
Tailor	Tega	
Taipan	Tenaka	
Taj	Teo Pepe	
Taja	Tequila	
Taka	Teresa	
Takai	Terry	Tilly
Tamea	Tess	Tim
Tammie	Tessa	Timmy
Tammy	Tessie	Timothy
Tamsin	Tessy	Tin Tin
Tamus	Tex	Tina
Tango	Texan	Tina Mia
Tania	Texas	Tincker
Tao	Thai	Tinkerbell
Tara	Thea	Tinks
Tarah	Thelma	Tinley
Tarka-Tu	Thom	Tinny
Tarra	Thomas	Tiny
Tarson	Thor	Tippie
Tas	Thrreebee	Tippy
Tasha	Thug	Tipsy
Tashi	Thunder	Tish
Tasman	Ti	Tisha
Tassie	Tia	Titan
Tasso	Tico	Titch
Tatunka	Tiddly	Titus
Tau	Tiff	Tobi
Tayla	Tiffany	Tobias Toby
Taylor	Tiger	Tochka
Tayo	Tigga	Toff
Tazzie	Tigger	Toffee
Tchalo	Tiggy	Toffy
Teba	Tiko	Togo
	Tillie	Tojo

Tollana
Tom
Tommy
Tonka
Tonkin
Tonto
Tootie Fruity
Tootsie
Toovy
Topaz
Toppa
Topsky
Topsy
Topuli
Topy
Tor
Tori
Toro
Tosh
Tosha
Totchka
Toto
Tous
Toushka
Toy
Trad
Treble
Trent
Trev
Trigger
Trio
Tripe
Tristram
Trixi
Trixie
Trudie
Trudy
Truffles

Tsar
Tuck
Tuffy
Tugbah
Tuggles
Tuk Tuk
Tuki
Tully
Tuppence
Tuppy
Tuskani
Tut
Twiggy
Twinkle
Twisty
Twit
Two
Twopence
Ty
Tyler
Tyrone
Tyrrells
Tyson
Tyson Fluffy
Tzar

V

Vamp
Vegemite
Velvet
Vesla
Victor
Victoria
Vienna
Viking
Villian
Vinnie-Sue
Virginia

Vitto
Voodoo
Vooki

W

Waggles
Waggs
Wagon
Waka
Waldo
Wally
Walter
Wanda
Wandjie
Waxer
Webster
Wendell
Wendy
Weris
Wesley
Whippy
Whiskey
Whitney
Whoopi
Whoopy
Wickerty Wack
Wilbur
Wilfred
William
Willie
Willy
Windsor
Windy
Wink
Winkie
Winnie
Winny
Winston

Woky
Wolf
Wolfgang
Wolfie
Wombat
Wombi
Womble
Woodstock
Woody
Woof
Woofa
Woolly
Wozzie
Wrigley

X
Xena
Xerxes

Y
Yamba
Yan
Yani
Yasmine

Yeni
Yindi
Yindy
Yo
Yoda
Yogi
Yoko
Yum Yum

Z
Za Za
Zaar
Zac
Zach
Zachary
Zack
Zahn
Zane
Zaniel
Zap
Zara
Zaras
Zebedee
Zebediah

Zedd
Zen
Zena
Zeno
Zero
Zeus
Ziff
Zig
Zig Zag
Ziggy
Zilla
Zimi
Zippy
Zita
Zodiac
Zoe
Zola
Zolly
Zorro
Zoul
Zox
Zudnik
Zugli
Zulu

CATS

A
A C
A J
Abba
Abbey
Abbie
Abbott
Abby
Abigail
Ace

Ada
Adelaide
Addie
Adeva
Adjani
Aerial
Aero
Aicha
Akina
Al

Alberquerque
Albert
Alberta
Alec
Alex
Alexander
Alexie
Alfie
Alfred
Ali

Ali Khan
Alice
Alike
Alinta
Allethea
Alley
Allie
Ama
Amah
Amanda
Amber
Ambrose
Amelia
Amon-Ra
Amy
Anastasia
Andretti
Andy
Angel
Angela
Angelica
Angelique
Angie
Angus
Anike
Anki
Anna
Annabella
Annabelle
Annastasia
Annie
Anooshka
Anouche
Antonina
Anuschka
Anzac
Aphro
Apollo

April
Arabella
Archie
Arfer
Argenta
Argyle
Arjuna
Armaggedon
Arnie
Arnold
Arpege
Art
Arthur
Ash
Ashanti
Asher
Ashleigh
Ashok
Asja
Aspen
Atticus
Attilla
Audrey
Augustus
Auriel
Aurora
Aussie
Autumn
Ayla
Azja
Azuree
Azzaza

B
B B
B T
Baba
Babagnoosh

Babe
Babette
Babs
Baby
Babygirl
Bacchus
Bach
Bachi
Baci
Bagel
Baggins
Baggy
Bagheera
Bailey
Baileys
Baja
Bajimby
Baldrick
Bali
Ballou
Bam-Bam
Bambi
Ban Ban
Bandit
Bangles
Banjo
Barnabus
Barnaby
Barney
Barnie
Barry
Bart
Basil
Basilcat
Batcat
Batman
Baxter
Bazer

NAME YOUR PET!

Bazil	Bib	Blitzen
Bazza	Bibby	Blossom
Bea	Bibs	Blossum
Beam	Biddy	Blue
Beans	Biff	Blue Boy
Bear	Biffy	Bluebell
Beatrice	Big Black Cat	Bluey
Beau	Big Doodie	Bo
Beau Beau	Big Puss	Bo Bo
Beau K	Biggles	Bob
Beauchamp	Billy	Bobbie
Becky	Billy Boy	Bobby
Bee	Bijoux	Bobby Sox
Bee Gee	Bilbo	Bobcat
Beeswax	Bill	Bodie
Bega	Billie	Bogart
Bella	Billy	Bogey
Belle	Bimba	Boj
Bells	Bimbo	Bondi
Ben	Bindi	Bondy
Benjamin	Bindy	Boney
Benji	Bing	Bonnie
Benny	Bingo	Bonny
Benoir	Binky	Boof
Benson	Binti	Boofhead
Bentley	Biscuit	Boofie
Berber	Biskit	Boofy
Bernie	Black	Booker
Berry	Black Baby	Booky
Bert	Black Cat	Boots
Bertie	Black Jack	Bootsie
Bertolli	Black White	Booty
Bess	Blackett	Boral
Bessie	Blackie	Boris
Betsy	Blackout	Boston
Betty	Blacky	Boswell
Bianca	Blanche	Bow
Bianco	Blinkey	Boy

Boynton
Boz
Bracken
Brandy
Brat
Brat Cat
Brian
Bright Eyes
Brin
Brioche
Bronson
Bronte
Brookie
Brown Cat
Brownie
Bruce
Bruiser
Brummel
Bruno
Bruser
Brutus
Bub
Bubble
Bubbles
Bubi
Bud
Buddy

Buffy
Buggles
Buik
Bulla
Bullwinkle
Bully
Bumper
Bundle
Bundy
Bunny
Burnie
Burt
Bus
Busby
Buster
Busy
Butch
Butterball
Buttercup
Buttons
Buzz
Bwana
Byron

C
C
C For
C C
Cactus
Caddie
Caesar
Cagney
Cairo
Caitlin
Calico
Cally
Calvin
Calypso

Cameo
Campo
Candy
Canleigh
Cappi
Cappuccino
Cara
Caramel
Carita
Carlos
Carlos Felipe
Carlton
Carma
Carmen
Caroline
Carrington
Casablanca
Casey
Casio
Casper
Cass
Cassidy
Cassie
Cassiopeia
Cassius
Cassper
Cassy
Cat
Catastrophe
Cat-Balloo
Caveat
Cecil
Cecilia
Ceena
Celine
Cephy
Cfor
Chablis

35

NAME YOUR PET!

Chad
Chadders
Chairo
Chalu
Champas
Champers
Champus
Chan
Chanel
Chanette
Channel
Charles
Charley
Charlie
Charlie Brown
Charlie Gray
Charlotte
Chas
Chat
Chatte
Chatters
Che Che Bella
Checkers
Cheeky
Cheetah
Chelsea
Cherie
Cherrie
Cherry
Cherub
Chester
Chevy
Chewbacca
Chewy
Chi
Chi Chi
Chilla
Chilli

Chin Chin
China
Chintz
Chip
Chips
Chiquilin
Chisel
Chloe
Chocci
Chocky
Choco
Chocolate
Chocolate
  Cake
Chole
Chomsky
Choo Choo
Chopin
Chots
Chow
Chrissy
Christabel
Christie
Christine
Christy
Chubbs
Chucky
Chungfu
Church
Cicada
Cimba
Cinamon
Cinderella
Cinders
Cindy
Cinna
Cinnamon
Cisca

Cisco
Ciska
Cita
Cladagh
Clarence
Claude
Claudius
Claw
Clawed
Clayton
Cleo
Cleopatra
Clicquot
Clinton
Clive
Clix
Clouseau
Clyde
Clydell
Cobber
Cobweb
Coca Cola
Coco
Coconut
Cody
Cognac
Cointreau
Cola
Collingwood
Combat
Concerto
Consuela
Cooee
Cookie
Cool
Copper
Corby
Corey

Cori
Corky
Corrie
Cosby
Cosima
Cosmo
Cosworth
Couch
Cougall
Crackers
Crazy
Cricket
Cristobel
Critter
Croissant
Crumble
Crusty
Crystal
Cuddle Pie
Cuddles
Cuff
Curtis
Curtly
Cush
Custard
Cutie
Cy
Cybil
Czar

D

D J
Daffy
Daisy
Dakota
Daks
Danny
Darcy

Darlene
Darling
Dartagnan
Dave
David
Deana
Deanna
Debonair
Dela
Delice
Dennis
Desi
Devil
Dewi
Di Di
Diablo
Diamond
Diana
Diasy
Digger
Dillie
Dillon
Dingo
Dinky
Diousse
Dippy
Dolly
Dolly Varden
Domingo
Domus
Donna
Donut
Doodie
Dooey
Dopey
Dorcas
Doris
Dorothy

Dot
Dotty
Douglas
Drummer
Ducatti
Dudley
Duffy
Duk
Dusky
Dusty
Dweezel
Dylan

E

E T
Eartha
Eartha Kitt
Ebby
Ebee
Ebony
Eddie
Eddy
Eden
Edward
Edwina
Eedra
Einstein
Electra
Eleesha
Eli
Elijah
Elizabeth
Elle
Ellie
Elliot
Elly
Elmo
Elmo Arnold

Els
Elsa
Elsie
Elvis
Emby
Emerald
Emily
Emma
Emma Bronte
Emma Peel
Emmy
Enya
Eponine
Eric
Erik
Ernest
Errol
Eso
Essy
Estelle
Etc
Everest

F

F 19
Fang
Farrah
Fat Cat
Fatso
Felicity
Felix
Feliz
Femmie
Fergie
Fergus
Festy
Fidel
Fifi

Figaro
Fin
Finn
Finnigan
Fire & Ice
Fitzy
Flee
Fletch
Floosie
Flora
Flossie
Flossy
Floyd
Fluff
Fluffy
Fonzie
Foofoo
Foss
Fossey
Foster
Foufette
Fove
Fox
Foxie
Foxy
Fozdik
Fozzie
Frances
Frangipani
Frank
Franki
Frankie
Franklin
Franky
Frascati
Frazer
Freckles
Fred

Freda
Freddo
Freddy
Freya
Freycinet
Friday
Friska
Frisky
Fritz
Frusty
Fu
Fudge
Fuschia

G

Galaderiel
Garfield
Garp
Garry
Gary
Gatto Pardo
Gemma
Geordie
George
Georgie
Georgina
Gerald

Geri
Gerry
Gertie
Gertrude
Gfor
Gi Gi
Gibbitty
Gibs
Gidget
Gilbert
Gina
Gindy
Ging
Ginge
Ginger
Ginger Abby
Ginger Cat
Ginger Meggs
Ginger Mickey
Ginger Paws
Gingus
Gingy
Ginney
Ginny
Giovanni
Gismo
Gizmo
Gizzy
Gnocci
Gobelino
Gogo
Goldie
Goldilocks
Golly
Gomez
Googy Egg
Goose
Gordon

Gordon
Benett
Grace
Gracie
Graham
Granite
Gregory
Gremlin
Greta
Grey
Greymalken
Grimaldi
Grotty
Gucci
Guinness
Gulliver
Gumby
Gummi
Gumnut
Gus
Gypsy
Gysmo

H
H G
Haggis
Haju
Halley
Hamish
Hamlet
Hana
Hank
Hannah
Hara
Harlem
Harley
Harold
Harrier

Harriet
Harriette
Harrison
Harry
Harvey
Hastings
Hattie
Hazel
Hector
Heidi
Hendo
Henritta
Henry
Herbert
Hercules
Hermes
Hero
Hexagon
Hilary
Hilda
Hildergard
Hitam
Hobbs
Hobi
Hobie
Holly
Honey
Horace
Horatio
Houdini
Hound
Hovie
Howard
Huang
Hugo
Humphey
Humphrey
Hungry

39

NAME YOUR PET!

I

Ichabod
Ilai
Inca
Indi
India
Indiana
Indra
Indy
Inky
Iris
Isaac
Isabel
Isabella
Isabelle
Isobella
Itchy
Itchy Boy
Ivo
Izzy

J

J D
Jaala
Jack
Jackson
Jacques
Jacquii
Jade
Jaffa
Jaguar
Jai
Jake
Jamal
Jamali
Jamie
Janey
Jango

Janis
Janx
Jaques
Jardy
Jasmin
Jasmine
Jason
Jasper
Jaxon
Jay
Jazz
Jean Clawed
  Belmondo
Jeannie
Jedda
Jellicoe
Jemima
Jemimah
Jemma
Jenny
Jeremiah
Jerlisa
Jerome
Jerry
Jess
Jesse
Jessica
Jessie
Jester
Jet
Jet Cat
Jethro
Jezabel
Jilly
Jim
Jimbi
Jiminy
Jimmy

Jindy
Jing
Jingles
Jo Jo
Joanne
Jock
Jodie
Joe
Joey
John
John Candy
Johnnie
Johnny
Johnson
Jolly
Jonsie
Jose
Josephine
Josh
Joshua
Josiah
Josie
Jossie
Juan
Juanita
Judy
Julia
Juliette
Julius

K

K 2
Ka
Kaffa
Kahlua
Kaitlyn
Kal
Kali

Kalib	Kins	Kymber
Kalua	Kipper	Kyra
Kami	Kippling	
Kanga	Kiri	**L**
Kao	Kirsten	L A
Karma	Kishma	Lady
Kashmir	Kissa	Lady Kathleen
Kasi	Kit	Lamington
Kate	Kitt	Lana
Katerina	Kitten	Langford
Katie	Kitty	Lara
Katina	Kitty Angel	Larry
Katja	Kitty Cat	Laser
Katmandu	Kitty Kat	Laura
Kato	Kitty Litter	Laurel
Katsu	Kiwi	Laxmi
Katy	Klaus	Layla
Kay	Knickers	Lea
Kay Dee	Knuckle	Leah
Kayja	Ko Ki	Leanna
Kazamir	Koko	Lear
Keiffer	Koshka	Ledge
Keira	Kotka	Leila
Keisha	Koto	Lelik
Kelly	Kotyk	Lenny
Ken	Kracker Jack	Leo
Ketty	Kratzerli	Leonie
Ketut	Krista	Leopard
Khan	Kristy	Leroy
Khani	Krystol	Lettie
Khasha	Kuching	Levi
Ki	Kucing	Levi-Rose
Killer	Kunta	Lewa
Kim	Kus Kus	Lewis
Kimba	Kusack	Lexi
Kimmy	Kushka	Lexy
Kinda	Kuss Kuss	Lia
Kingston	Kylah	Libby

Lickety
Licorice
Liesl
Lightning
Lil Pudd
Lila
Lilly
Ling
Ling Ling
Linus
Lion
Lisa
Little Cat
Little Diddle -
    King
Little Doodie
Little Girl
Little Guy
Little Kitty
Little Mittens
Little One
Little Puddy
Little Puss
Little Tabby
Littley
Lizzie
Lladro
Lloyd
Lodger
Logan
Loki
Lola
Lolita
Lolly
Lonely
Lonesome
Long Tail
Lord Angus

Lord
    Mackinnon
Lotte
Lotus
Lou
Louie
Louis
Louise
Lovey
Lowanna
Lowry
Loxy
Lucas
Luce
Lucille
Lucinda
Lucky
Lucky Tom
Lucy
Luda
Lui
Luka
Luke
Luli
Lulu
Lutz

M
M C
M P
Mabilu
Mac
Macduff
Macina
Macro
Mad
Madali
Madam

Maddie
Maddy
Madge
Madison
Madonna
Maggie
Maggie May
Magnum
Magnus
Mahjong
Mai Tai
Maisie
Maisy
Maki
Mallet
Malmi
Mambo
Mami
Manchy
Mandarin
Mandarley
Mandu
Mandy
Mango
Manly
Mannix
Manuel
Mao
Mao Mao
Maow
Mapp
Marco
Marcus
Marqwa
Marion
Marley
Marlow
Marmaduke

Marmalade	Meggy	Mimi
Marmite	Megs	Min
Marnix	Megsy	Mince
Marta	Meia	Minchinbury
Martha	Mein	Mindi
Martisse	Meisje	Mindy
Marty	Melanie	Ming
Marvey	Melanzane	Ming Ming
Mary	Melba	Mingus
Marylyn	Melbourne	Mini
Marzipan	Meow	Mink
Mascara	Mephisto	Minka
Maschka	Mercedes	Minke
Mason	Mergatroyd	Minkey
Matilda	Merinda	Minkie
Matt	Merlie	Minky
Matty	Merlin	Minney
Mau Mau	Merlina	Minnie
Maude	Merp	Minnie Mouse
Maudie	Mia	Minou
Maurice	Micah	Minsky
Mave	Michael	Minstral
Maverick	Michelle	Mintie
Max	Michi	Minty
Maxine	Micki	Minxie
Maxwell	Micky	Mischa
Maxy	Middy	Mischief
Mayake	Midnight	Mischka
Maybel	Midy	Mish
May-Lee	Miffy	Misha
Maynard	Mike	
Mayo	Mikey	
Mctavish	Mikki	
Meeko	Mildew	
Meg	Miles	
Meggie	Millie	
Meggs	Milly	
Meggsie	Milo	

43

Mishca
Mishi
Mishka
Mishkar
Mishy
Miss Prissy
Missie
Mission
Missy
Mist
Mista
Mister
Misty
Misty Puss
Mitsu
Mitsy
Mitty
Mitze
Mitzi
Mitzy
Mo
Moe
Moet
Moey
Mogg
Moggie
Moggy
Mogsy
Moisha
Mojo
Mollie
Molly
Mon
Mona
Monday
Monet
Mongee
Monie

Monkey
Monnie
Monster
Montana
Monte
Monty
Monza
Moo
Mooch
Mook
Moonbeam
Moose
Mooshi
Mooty
Moppet
Morag
Morbell
Morgan
Moriyz
Morris
Morse
Morse Code
Morticha
Morticia
Mortisha
Mosby
Moses
Mosey
Moss
Moth
Mother
Mother Cat
Motley
Mouse
Mousey
Mouska
Mousse
Mowgli

Mozart
Mozzi
Mozzie
Mr Border
Mr Cat
Mr Cheecky
Mr Chloe
Mr Conan
Mr Grace
Mr Herriot
Mr Mcphee
Mr Puddy
Mr Smif
Mr Stevens
Mr Stripy
  Pants
Mr T
Mr Tom Wong
Mrs Bones
Mrs Cleo Puss
Mrs Puss
Mudcrab
Muff
Muffin
Muffins
Muffy
Mufti
Mugwai
Mulberry
Mulder
Mum Puss
Munchie
Munchkin
Mung
Mungo
Muppy
Murgatroyd
Murph

Murphy
Musetta
Musette
Mushie
Mushka
Mushroom
Mushy
Musket
Mutley
Mutt
Myrrh
Mystique
Mystra

N

Nala
Nancy
Nannuk
Napoleon
Natasha
Nathan
Nathaniel
Natsu
Naughty
Navi
Necka
Necki
Nefertiti
Neffa
Neil
Neischa
Neisha
Neko
Nelson
Nermal
Nero
Nessie
Nessy

Netty
Neungy
Nicheka
Nichi
Nicki
Nicky
Nicole
Nijinski
Nike
Nikita
Nim
Nimue
Nina
Ning
Nini
Ninja
Nippity
Nishi
Niska
Noddy
Noisette
Noki
Noni
Noody
Nori
Norm
Norman
Nouscha
Nudge
Numpsi
Nushka
Nutmeg
Nuts
Nutty

O

Oberon
Obi

Ocho
Octo
Odie
Odin
Oki
Olive
Oliver
Olivia
Oli
Ollie
Olly
Oops
Oopsy
Ophelia
Ophie
Opie
Orange
Orange Boy
Orlando
Oscar
Oska
Othello
Ottie
Otto
Owl
Oz
Ozzie
Ozzy

P

P C
Pablo
Paddles
Paddo
Paddy
Paddy Fin
Pagan
Paint Tin

45

NAME YOUR PET!

Paladin	Pedro	Piddles
Paloma	Peewee	Pie
Panda	Peggy	Piffany
Pantha	Pele	Pillin
Panther	Pelham	Pimms
Paris	Pendragon	Ping
Parker	Penelope	Ping Pong
Pasha	Penny	Pinocchio
Pastel	Pepe	Pip
Patch	Pepi	Pipi
Patches	Peppa	Pippa
Patchy	Pepper	Pippi
Patrick	Peppi	Pippin
Patsy	Peppy	Pippy
Pattie	Percy	Pitch
Paul	Peri	Pittzi
Pavarotti	Perina	Pixel
Pavlovich	Perry	Pixie
Peaches	Persephone	Playful
Peachy	Persia	Plunkett
Pear	Pesh	Pluto
Pearl	Pesto	Pod
Pearly	Pesty	Podgy
Pebbles	Pete	Pokey
Pedra	Peter	Pokie
	Peter Pan	Polar
	Peter Polly	Polly
	Petite Toutou	Polo
	Petunia	Poncie
	Phantom	Pone
	Pharoah	Pong
	Philamena	Pongo
	Phoebe	Ponti
	Phoenix	Poo
	Phremy	Pooch
	Piatza	Pooh
	Picasso	Pookie
	Pickles	Pooky

46

Popcorn
Poppet
Poppy
Popsy
Porridge
Porscha
Portia
Poss
Possum
Pounce
Povorino
Prancer
Pratchett
Pretzel
Primrose
Prince
Princess
Priscilla
Prowler
Prudence
Prufrock
Psyche
Puce
Pucin
Puck
Pud
Pudding
Puddles
Puddup
Puddy
Puddy Cat
Puddy Puddy
Pudgie
Puff
Puffin
Pug
Pugsly
Puhd

Pumpkin
Punter
Purcy
Purdie
Purdita
Pure White
Purrdy
Purrsephone
Purrseus
Purrson
Pushka
Pushkin
Pushush
Pushy
Puska
Puss
Puss In Boots
Puss Puss
Pussca
Pusscat
Pussi
Pussum
Pussy
Pussy Cooma
Pussy Poppett
Pussy Willow
Pussycat
Pussyfoot
Pusvwa
Puto
Puzzle
Pye

Q

Quality
Queenie
Quincy
Quiver

R

Ra
Rabbit
Radar
Rafeke
Raffles
Rahjie
Railene
Rain
Rainbow
Raj
Rajah
Ralph
Rama
Rambo
Rameses
Ramius
Rana
Randi
Ranee
Rangi
Rangoon
Rani
Raoul
Raphael
Rascal
Rasmus
Rat
Ratty
Ratu
Raven
Raynor
Raz
Rebecca
Rebel
Reebok
Reggae
Reggie

NAME YOUR PET!

Remus	Rosko	Sallyann
Rex	Rowdy	Salt & Pepper
Rhama	Rowland	Sam
Richard	Roxanne	Samantha
Richenda	Ru	Samba
Richie	Rubens	Samisen
Rick	Ruby	Sammy
Ricki	Rudi	Sampson
Rimini	Rudy	Samson
Rin Tin	Ruffles	Samuel
Rip Rak	Rufus	Samui
Ripley	Rugger	San
Ripples	Rumples	Sandi
River	Rumpole	Sandy
Robin	Rumpus	Sangupor
Robyn	Rupert	Sansha
Rocket	Rupes	Santa
Rocklilly	Ruprect	Sapphie
Rocky	Rushkin	Sapphire
Rodger	Ruska	Sappho
Rodney	Ruski	Sara
Roger	Russkie	Sarah
Roland	Rusty	Sardi
Roly		Sascha
Romeo	**S**	Sash
Rommel	S B	Sasha
Romulus	Sabella	Sassy
Ronnie	Saber	Satchmo
Roo	Sable	Saul
Rory	Sabre	Sauren
Rose	Sabrina	Sausage
Rose Petals	Sacha	Saxon
Rosebud	Sachi	Sayam
Rosencrantz	Sade	Scabby
Rosetta	Sadie	Scamp
Rosey	Sage	Scampy
Rosi	Saki	Scardy
Rosie	Sally	Scarlett

Scarab
Schamus
Schnule
Schon
Schubert
Scilla
Scooter
Scotty
Scrap
Scratch
Scratchy
Scruff
Scruffy
Scrumpy
Scully
Scwuffy
Sean
Seaview
Sebastian
Seeto
Selena
Selina
Serano
Seymour
Shackera
Shadow
Shakespeare
Shakira
Shakti
Shaman
Shamar
Shammy
Shamus
Shan
Shani
Shannon
Shapachou
Shar

Sharne
Shashe
Shattwo
Shazam
Sheba
Sheema
Sheila
Shelford
Shelley
Shelly
Shenka
Sherman
Shigh
Shimbi
Shimi
Shiralee
Shirley
Shiroi
Shiva
Shmee
Shminki
Shmitten
Shoki
Shortie
Shula
Shushi
Si
Siam
Sian
Sibalius
Sid
Sidney
Siggi
Silky
Silly
Silver
Silvester
Silvy

Simba
Simby
Simon
Simone
Sinbad
Sirach
Sirkit
Siska
Skeeta
Skelm
Sketty
Skinny
Skippy
Skisto
Skitso
Skittles
Skitty Cat
Skitzo
Sky
Skye
Slinky
Slivia
Smakka
Small Fry
Smidgen
Smokey
Smokey Bear
Smooch
Smoose
Smudge
Snippets
Snitty
Snookie
Snooky
Snoops
Snoopy
Snootzie
Snorkel

NAME YOUR PET!

Snow	Spider	Storm
Snow Beau	Spike	Strawberry
Snowball	Spikey	Stray Mum
Snowflake	Spinach	Streaker
Snow White	Spinner	Strumpet
Snowy	Spirit	Stumpy
Snuffles	Spit	Stupe
Snuffy	Splash	Stupid
Snugglepot	Splotch	Su Su
Snuggler	Spock	Sugar
Snuggles	Spook	Suki
Sobella	Spooky	Su-Lin
Socks	Spot	Sula
Soda	Spotty	Sultan
Soe	Sprocket	Sumba
Solomon	Spud	Sumo
Sonia	Spunky	Sunny
Sonny	Sqeaky	Sunshine
Soo	Squadgy	Surfy
Sook	Squeak	Sushi
Sooki	Squeaker	Susie
Sooky	Squeaky	Suvi
Sootica	Squib	Suzie
Sootie	Squid	Suzuka
Sooty	Squidgy	Suzy
Sophie	Squiggy	Sweet Emma
Souffle	Squizzie	Sweet Pea
Sox	Squizzy	
Soxie	Stanley	
Soxy	Star	
Space Cat	Stella	
Sparkles	Stetson	
Sparky	Steve	
Spats	Stimpy	
Spatz	Stinky	
Spaz	Stjohn	
Speedo	Stokes	
Speedwell	Stomper	

Sweetie Puss
Swift
Sybella
Sybil
Syd
Sydney
Sylvesta
Sylvester
Sylvia
Sylvie
Sylvy
Syninan
Szupi

T
T C
Tabatha
Tabby
Tabby Man
Tabby White
Tablet
Taboo
Tabs
Tabsy
Tacha
Tacking
Taffy
Tahnee
Tahsha
Tai
Taipan
Taj
Taki
Tamara
Tami
Tamiko
Tamil
Tamina

Tammy
Tamsen
Tanamera
Tandy
Tang
Tangerine
Tangles
Tango
Tani
Tania
Taniko
Tanj-It
Tanka
Tansy
Tanzy
Tao
Tara
Targa
Tarquin
Tash
Tasha
Tassie
Tates
Tattles
Tawny Tesse
Tawny Tikee
Tawny Tillee
Taylor
Taz
Tazi
Teaka
Te-Amo
Ted
Teddy
Teddy Bear
Teeny
Tela
Tercia

Terry
Tesha
Tess
Tessa
Tessie
Tex
Texas
Thaidy
Thaie
Thani
The Butler
Thea
Thelma
Thirteen
Thomas
Thomasina
Thumper
Thunder
Tia
Tibby
Ticky
Tico
Tiddler
Tiddles
Tiddly Pom
Tierney
Tiffany
Tiga
Tiger
Tiger Puss
Tigga
Tigger
Tigger Puss
Tiggs
Tiggy
Tigsey
Tiki
Tikka

NAME YOUR PET!

Tilin
Tillie
Tilly
Tim
Timmy
Timothy
Tin Tin
Tina
Tini
Tinka
Tinker
Tinkerbell
Tinky
Tinsel
Tiny
Tip
Tippets
Tippi
Tippy
Tipsy
Tira
Tish
Tisha
Tishka
Titch
Titch Too
Tituba
Titus
Tobias
Toby
Toddles
Toddy
Toffee
Toffilees
Toga
Tokolosh
Tolstoy
Tom

Tom Kitten
Tom Tom
Tomcat
Tomkinson
Tomkit
Tommy
Tonk
Tonka
Tonto
Tooley
Toot
Tootie
Toots
Tootsie
Top Cat
Topaz
Topsy
Tora
Tortie
Tortise
Tortoi
Torty
Tory
Tosca
Tosh
Toshi
Touche
Toxo
Toy
Toya
Trashy
Trebor
Trelawney
Trevour
Trigger
Trini
Trinket
Tristan

Trixie
Truffles
Tsien
Tugger
Tujo
Tuna
Tunguska
Tuppence
Tuppenny
Tuppy
Turbo
Tuscot
Tutan
Tux
Tuxy
Tweedle Dum
Tweety
Twiddle
Twiddle Dee
Twig
Twiggy
Twinkle
Twinkles
Twinky
Ty
Tyla
Tzar

V

Vahine
Valentine
Valentino
Vegemite
Venus
Veronica
Vesta
Victor
Victoria

Vince
Vincent
Vinnie
Violet
Viv
Voila

W
Waif
Walgett
Wally
Wanda
Warren
Watson
Wayne
Weadle
Wesley
Wheely
Whelan
Whiffy
Whinger
Whingy
Whiskas
Whiskers
Whiskey
Whisky
Whisper
White Cat
Whitey
Whitney
Whoopi
Wicky Woo
Wilbur
Wilbur-Puss
William
Willie
Willow
Willy

Wilma
Wincy
Windy
Winkie
Winkle
Winnie
Winnipeg
Winston
Winter
Wolf
Wolfgang
Wombat
Woody
Woos
Woosel
Woosie
Wooso
Worry
Worsel

X
Xanadu
Xanthor
Xie Xie

Y
Yana
Yang
Yani
Yashka
Yasmine
Yeti
Yo Yo
Yoda
Yodi
Yorick
Yoshi
Yum Yum

Z
Zac
Zach
Zachary
Zack
Zag
Zak
Zamandalay
Zamin
Zane
Zap
Zarlee
Zazu
Zeba
Zebedee
Zebie
Zelda
Zena
Zenzi
Zeus
Zi Zi
Zig
Ziggy
Zilog
Zinzan
Zip
Zipper
Zippy
Zodia
Zoe
Zoltan
Zonk
Zorro
Zsa Zsa
Zu Zu
Zulee
Zulu
Zumi

BIRDS

A
Alex
Alice
Andrew
Angel
Aussie

B
Baby
Barney
Basil
Be Be
Beasley
Beast
Beauty
Becky
Bella
Ben
Bernie
Bert
Bertie
Berzacle
B G
Bib
Bicky
Big Boy
Bill
Billy
Bing
Bird
Birdie
Birdy
Bismark
Blinky
Blue

Blue Boy
Bluey
Bob
Bobbie
Bobby
Boid
Bowie
Bub
Buba
Bubby
Bud
Buddie
Buddy
Budge
Budgie
Budgie Boy
Buster
Butch
Buttercup

C
Captain
Casper
Cassie
Cassy
Charlene
Charlie
Chatter Box
Cheeky
Cheeky Boy
Chester
Chilli
Chipper
Chips
Chirper

Chirpie
Chirpy
Chook
Chubby
Chuck
Chutney
Clancy
Cloudy
Clyde
Cockwa
Cocky
Coco
Coke
Coop
Corey
Corry
Crazy Joe
Crocka
Crystal

D
Daffodil
Di
Diana
Dick
Dicko
Douglas
Duck

E
Eli
Elwood
Embeau
Emma
Enoch

Enzo
Eric
Ernie

F
Fergie
Fester
Fivel
Fluffy
Franky
Fred
Freddy
Fudgie

G
Gallo
Garva
Georgie
Gertie
Goldie
Golgie
Gorgeous
Grey Girl
Gus

H
Harley
Haywire
Henny
Henrietta
Herbie
Hercules
Himogee
Hopper

I
Ickey
Iris

J
Jack
Jackson
Jade
Jaffa
Jambo
Jamie
Jammy
Jasmine
Jason
Jasper
Jeffrey
Jerry
Jessica
Jessie
Jill
Jimmy
Jock
Jodis
Joe
Joey
Jojo
Josephine
Juke
Julie
Juliette
Julio

K
K G
Kb
Kelly
Kirri

L
Lady Budgie
Larry
Laurel

Lennie
Lockey
Lotto
Lou Lou
Lucky
Luke

M
Mac
Macintosh
Maia
Marty
Marvin
Mary
Mask
Matey
Max
Maya
Mickey
Midge
Missy
Monty
Moon
Mouse
Mr Happy
Mr Universe
Mr Messy
Mrs B
Mrs Dickie
Mystery

N
Nakisha
Nipper
Noddy
Noel
Noha
Nudge

55

NAME YOUR PET!

O
Oleander
Opal
Oscar
Oskar
Ozzi

P
Parrot
Paton
Pavarotti
Peabody
Pebbles
Pedro
Peewee
Peggy
Peppi
Peppy
Pete
Peter
Petie
Phil
Philly
Pierre
Pinky
Pipi
Polly
Pooky
Popeye
Poppy
Pretty Boy
Prince
Punky
Puss Puss

Q
Quail
Quark

R
Racer
Rain
Reece
Regie
River
Robbie
Rocky
Roger
Romeo
Rooster
Rosie

S
Saffi
Sally
Sam
Sammy
Sandy
Sara
Scooby
Scruffy
Shade
Shannon
Sharon
Shay
Shen
Sherlock
Sid
Sidney
Silver
Sky
Sky Blue
Smithy
Snow
Snowy
Socrates
Sophie

Sparkey
Sparkle
Sparky
Spartacus
Specky
Spike
Spot
Steggles
Sue
Sunny
Sunshine
Swanee
Sweetheart
Sweetie Pie
Sweety
Sylvester

T
Tammy
Taryn
Ted
Tequila
The Boy
Thomas
Tiger
Tilly
Tim
Tipple
Toby
Toni
Toto
Tracey
Trouble
Turtledove
Tweetie
Tweety
Twitie Pie
Two Bob

V
Valentino

W
Wal

Waldo
Wally
Willie
William
Winnie

Woodstock

Z
Zac
Ziggy

RABBITS

A
Albert
Alexander
Angela
Angus

B
B1
B2
Baby
Baggins
Bella
Ben
Benjamin
Benny
Billy
Blackie
Blinkie
Bo
Bonnie
Boof
Buddy
Bugeyes
Buggs
Bugs
Bugsie
Bugsy
Bun Bun
Bunkins

Bunnies
Bunny
Bunnykins

C
Casper
Chalrina
Charlie
Charlotte
Cheeky
Chelsea
Chilli
Chippy
Cinders
Cindy
Claudette
Claudie
Clover
Coco
Coffey
Cooky
Cosmo
Cotton
Cuddles
Cuthbert

D
Daisy
Darling

Dinner
Dodger
Don
Dusty

E
Ebony
Einstein
Electra
Elsa
Emma

F
Fairy Floss
Felicity
Fiver
Flop
Flopsy
Flopsy Bunny
Flower
Fluffy
Fred
Frisky
Fuzzy

G
Georgina
Gladys
Grey Bunny

NAME YOUR PET!

Grey Ears

H
Hannah
Harvey
Honey
Honky
Hopper
Hoppity
Hoppy

I
Ice

J
Jack
Jackson
Jessica
Jessie
Joey
Jojoba
Joshua
Jumper
Junior

L
Lady
Light Spot
Lilly Beth
Loppy
Lucy
Lucy White
Lush

M
M J
Maddy
Max

Meeko
Midnight
Mikala
Mischief
Misty
Moose
Mountain Dew
Muffin
Muffy
Mummy

N
Nappy
Nibbles
Noddy

P
Patch
Pepe
Pepper
Peter
Pink Ears
Podge
Podges
Pooh Bear
Poppett
Posca

R
Rabb
Rabbie
Rabbit
Rabby
Rastus
Richie Rich
Roger
Romper
Ruby

Rumple
Rupert

S
Sarah
Sebastian
Sherbert
Shovon
Simba
Smokey
Smokie
Smudge
Sniffy
Snooks
Snoopy
Snow
Snow Boy
Snow White
Snowball
Snowdrop
Snowflake
Snowman
Snowy
Snuffles
Snuggles
Socksy
Sooty
Sparkle
Spot
Sprite

T
Tappy
Thumper
Tibby
Tickles
Tom
Twinkle

Twitch
Tyrone

V
Valentinni

Violet

W
Welly
Whitey

Wodger

Z
Zoomy
Zeno

GUINEA PIGS

A
Annabell

B
Baby
Ben
Blackie
Bow
Boyzai

C
Candy - Anna
Caramel
Casserole
Chestnut
Chloe
Chubbles
Clover
Coco
Cuddles

D
Daisy
Day & Night

F
Flopsie
Fluffy
Fudge

G
G Pig
George
Gerry
Grace
Gracey
Guinea
Guinea Mum
Guinea Pig

H
Harry
Herbert
Hermy
Honey
Hugo

J
J C
Jake

L
Lady
Licorice

M
Mate
Max
Nala

O
Otak

P
Penny
Peppy
Petal
Pinky
Prudence

R
Rebel
Ribbon
Rosie

S
Sarah
Scruffy
Sooty
Spike
Springtime
Squeaky
Squirrel

T
Tinker
Thunder
Tweedle Dee
Tweedle Dum

THE TOP 100

THE DOG TOP 100

Jessie	Tyson	George
Max	Harley	Millie
Sam	Billy	Rex
Zac	Ralph	Patch
Lucy	Rosie	Amber
Chloe	Coco	Scamp
Oscar	Cleo	Skye
Beau	Scruffy	Muffin
Ben	Harry	Sebastian
Charlie	Tessa	Henry
Toby	Kelly	Mischa
Sasha	Cassie	Katie
Jake	Missy	Penny
Molly	Tammy	Sooty
Sally	Jasper	Muffy
Holly	Lady	Leroy
Bella	Cindy	Milo
Bonnie	Tara	Hamish
Sophie	Puppy	Teddy
Jack	Heidi	Duke
Zoe	Buffy	Spike
Sandy	Barney	Bundy
Tess	Gypsy	Bess
Honey	Ziggy	Snowy
Rocky	Brandy	Bo
Jedda	Bonny	Kim
Bear	Basil	Gus
Misty	Jackson	Peppi
Rusty	Jessica	Angus
Daisy	Jasmine	Chester
Sheba	Jemma	Fred
Monty	Emma	Matilda
Buster	Lucky	
Jess	Winnie	

THE CAT TOP 100

Misty
Tiger
Oscar
Sam
Max
Coco
Lucy
Missy
Sooty
Puss
Smokey
Kitten
Chloe
Tigger
Charlie
Muffin
Ginger
Toby
Cleo
Cat
Kitty
Blackie
Tom
Monty
Tabatha
Felix
Sox
Sophie
Fluffy
Sasha
Zoe
Thomas
Daisy
Jack

Jasmine
Cindy
Tammy
Milo
Tabby
Minnie
Casper
Smudge
Bonnie
Tinkerbell
Fred
Mickey
Sebastian
Samantha
Molly
Tasha
Muffy
Sally
Sheba
Pussy
Leo
Suki
Mischa
Bella
Phoebe
Rosie
Spike
Sammy
Kimba
Princess
T C
Boris
Mitzi
Honey

Harley
Harry
Jessica
Phantom
Buster
Amber
Simba
Sylvester
Ralph
Claude
Moet
Pebbles
Jessie
Basil
Snowy
Lily
Ming
Ben
Poppy
Megs
Millie
Midnight
Murphy
Ziggy
Benny
Tommy
George
Pixie
Mimi
Willy
Sarah
Lilly

THE BIRD TOP 40

Bird
Bluey
Billy
Sam
Buddy
Charlie
Fred
Tweetie
Pretty Boy
Harley
Peter
Bill
Bub
Cocky

Sweetheart
Rosie
Sparky
Snowy
Birdie
Joey
Max
Tweety
Lucky
Rocky
Jimmy
Joe
Buttercup
Jack

Hercules
Herbie
Casper
Sammy
Clyde
Romeo
Peggy
Georgie
Mary
Popeye
Missy
Pipi

THE RABBIT TOP 40

Rabbit
Bunny
Flopsy
Thumper
Bugsy
Roger
Smokey
Nibbles
Snow
Whitey
Twinkle
Muffin
Jessie
Smudge
Bun Bun
Snuggles
Buggs

Lucy
Blackie
Spot
Clover
Misty
Felicity
Frisky
Einstein
Ebony
Emma
Dusty
Don
Hoppity
Dinner
Darling
Hoppy
Daisy

Cuthbert
Cuddles
Dodger
Flopsy Bunny
Grey Ears
Guinea

THE GUINEA PIG TOP 40

Guinea
Guinea Pig
George
G Pig
Clover
Guinea Mum
Gracey
Grace
Gerry
Fudge
Fluffy
Day & Night
Annabell
Coco

Hermy
Chubbles
Chloe
Chestnut
Casserole
Candy - Anna
Boyzai
Bow
Blackie
Ben
Baby
Cuddles
Peppy
Tweedle Dee

Thunder
Squirrel
Squeaky
Springtime
Spike
Sooty
Scruffy
Sarah
Rosie
Ribbon
Rebel
Licorice

NAMES BY BREED

DOGS

AFGHAN CROSS
Kelly
Totto

AFGHAN HOUND
Affie
Alex
Debbie
Ginger
Zara

AIREDALE CROSS
Beau
Missy

AIREDALE TERRIER
Abby
Blossom
Boris
Charlotte
Emily
Finn Mccool
Harold
Jack
Max
Milo

Misty
Monty
Otis
Penelope
Rufus
Sally
Sophie

AKITA
Chao Ren
Tosha

ALASKAN MALAMUTE
Aleutia
Arizona
Barney
Bear
Boston
Chinook
Conan
Devil
Harley
Keesha
Layla
Luca
Luna
Meka
Misk
Mischa
Misty
Mr Mcgoo
Nanaque
Nanuq
Ned

Phantom
Sakima
Shoshone
Stroka
Tenaka

AMERICAN COCKER
Chip
Inky

AMERICAN STAFFORD-SHIRE
Stella

ANATOLIAN SHEPHERD
Angus

AUSTRALIAN CATTLE DOG
Angus
Bandit
Barney
Belle
Bess
Bill
Billy
Black Night
Blanche
Blue
Blue Nell
Bluey
Bobby
Boner

Bonnie	Gus	Mingus
Bonny	Gyp	Misty
Boss	Gypsy	Mitzie
Bowie	Hannah	Nancy
Bozo	Harley	Nathaniel
Bud	Harry	Paris Texas
Bundy	Hawk	Patch
Buster	Hoges	Patchy
C D	Indi	Pippa
Casey	Indiana	Ralph
Cedar	Indigo	Ramses
Charly	Jack	Rani
Cinders	Jackson	Rastus
Cindy	Jana	Red
Clancy	Jay	Reggae
Cleo	Jedda	Rex
Cobar	Jeff	Rocky
Cooee	Jess	Roland
Crash	Jesse	Rosie
Daisy	Jessi	Roxanne
Dana	Jessica	Sally
Danny	Jessie	Sari
Diesel	Jimmy	Sasha
Digger	Joey	Scamp
Ding	Judith	Sheba
Dozer	K T	Skyblue
Dugan	Lady	Smokey
Dutch	Leroy	Storm
Eli	Levi	Streuth
Eureka	Lottie	Stubby
Fifty	Magnum	Suzie
Flash	Mandy	Swag
Foxy	Matilda	Swampy
Frank	Max	T-Bone
George	Maxine	Tara
Gilbert	Megsie	Ted
Ginger	Miki	Tega
Godzilla	Mincer	Tess

NAME YOUR PET!

Tessie
Tex
Thea
Toby
Toto
Trad
Tyrone
Tyson
Wally
Wandjie
Waxer
Weris
Whiskey
William
Yindy
Zac
Ziff

AUSTRALIAN
KELPIE
Amy
Arkie
Ben
Bonney
Brandy
Brumby
Candy
Chad
Cilla
Cindy
Defa
Digger
Dorrie
Dusty
Dutchie
Ebony
Emma
Flynn

Foxy
Gum Nuts
Harry
Jack
Jake
Jasmine
Jedda
Jeddah
Jessica
Joey
Kelly
Kibble
King
Lucky
Lushka
Max
Milo
Minnie
Mouse
Ned
Nugget
Pepe
Ponsonby
Raz
Reuben
Rocky
Rosie
Rustina
Rusty
Saavik
Sally
Sambucca
Samson
Sascha
Sheba
Shep
Susie
Tassie

Tau
Teddy
Tequila
Toby
Winnie
Woody
Zac
Zena
Zippy

AUSTRALIAN
SILKY CROSS
Abu
Arnie
Barnsy
Beau
Bella
Benjy
Bobby
Bubbles
Buddy
Chelsea
Cully
Evie
Georgi
Gigi
Jasper
Jonte
Lady
Lucy
Lucy Brown
Midge
Misty
Molly
Muffy
Pete
Puppy
Ralph

Sam
Scruffy
Snuffy
Sophie
Susie
Tammy
Teddy
Tiff
Toby
Tom
Twiggy
Wagon
Zac

**AUSTRALIAN
SILKY**
Basil
Becci
Ben
Benjamin
Benji
Biddy
Billy
Blackie
Blue
Bonnie
Bonza
Brillow
Chloe
Cindy

Cougar
Cyndi
Daisy
Dimpy
Emi
Escher
Fabian
Floppy
Foxy
Gigi
Gypsy
Hannah
Harvey
Hercules
Jesse
Jessie
Jessoe
Jodi
Jodie
Jody
Katie
Katy
Kim
Lexie
Lucky
Mac
Mackie
Mandy
Matey
Max
Maxine
Mickey
Midge
Mindy
Minska
Mischa
Missy
Mitzi

Molly
Morgan
Muffin
Muffy
Munchkin
Nell
Nelson
Otto
Penny
Peta
Pippi
Poco
Rascal
Ricky Lee
Rosie
Ruby
Sally
Sam
Sandy
Scamp
Scampi
Scout
Scruffy
Sheena
Sherry
Simba
Sonet
Sooty
Sophie
Spike
Spud
Tammie
Tassie
Tess
Tobias
Horatio
  Nelson
Toby

Tom
Toto
Tuppence
Willy

AUSTRALIAN TERRIER

Ali
Aussie
Basil
Ben
Benny
Blossum
Bobby
Buffy
Chloe
Crystal
Fritz
Ginger
Grace
Harry
Jack
Jenna
Jester
Jimmy
Lexie
Lucy
Maddi
Matilda
Max
Midge
Misty
Mitzy
Mollie
Munchkin
Ned
O D
Offie

Oskar
Oz
Peppa
Peppi
Roger
Rosie
Rudi
Sam
Samson
Sasha
Scamp
Smiggin
Sydney
Terry
Tiger
Tina
Tinkerbell
Toby
Trixie
Waka
Zoe

AUSTRALIAN TERRIER CROSS

Benji
Chloe
Connie
Fang
Fluffy
Georgie
Laddie
Lucy
Mr Mush
Sam
Scarlet
Teddy
Willie
Zac

BASENJI

Ninja
Pippa
Rudi
Samuri
Zac

BASSET HOUND

Buster
Fred
Pedro
Rosie
Sebastian
Tia

BEAGLE

Alexander
Alice
Andy
Balto
Barney
Beattie
Bently
Bernie
Bertie
Biggles
Bill
B J
Bob
Bonnie
Boots
Boz
Bozley
Caesar
Cammy
Cissy
Dax
Dozer

Harley
Harry
Henderson
Hudson
Jaffa
Jake
Janey
Jemma
Jenna
Jessie
Jessie Belle
Jester
Kali
Kasper
Kelly
Kushla
Lucy
Luther
Matrix
Max
Molly
Moritz
Mr Biggles
Murphy
Nellie
Newton
Oscar
Paddles
Penny
Prince
Rex
Roxi
Rusty
Sally
Sheba
Sissy
Snoopy
Snuffy

Sumo
Toby
Tom

BEAGLE CROSS
Buffy
Cleo
Lucy
Missy
Molly
Pugzly
Pumpkin
Sox
Suzy

BEARDED COLLIE
Basil
Bess
Brooke
Echo
Jackson
Jeanne
Katie
Kelly
Muffin
Paddy
Phantom
Robbie

BEARDED COLLIE CROSS
Bessy
Lucy

BEDLINGTON TERRIER
Blast
Jaegar

Topsy

BELGIAN SHEPHERD DOG
Bellejovi
Chip
Duff
Kimba
Nonya
Serge
Sheba

BERNESE MOUNTAIN DOG
Rosti
Sebastian

BICHON FRISE
Anna
Ari
Arnold
Baron
Bella
Bess
Binky
B J
Bliss
Blossom
Bows
Brandy
Bruto
Cantona
Charlotte
Chloe
Christen
Claude
Coco
Cuddles

71

NAME YOUR PET!

Daisy
Duchess
Dudley
Duncan
Ellie
Georgia
Gizmo
Heidi
Hioni
Holly
Honey
Isis
Jasmine
Jason
Jasper
Katie
Kevin
Lilie
Lilly
Louis
Maddie
Major
Mattie
Micolee
Mikki
Miklmas
Millie
Monique
Monty
Moushka
Muffett
Penny
Ponti
Poppy
Pup
Rockie
Sam
Samantha

Shardi
Sid
Snegi
Snowy
Snugglepot
Sooty
Strudel
Sugar
Summer
Tas
Teddy
Tiffany
Toby
Tuppy
Winston

BICHON FRISE
CROSS
Buffy
Chloe
Monty
Rosie
Tess
Tuppy

BLOOD-HOUND
Emmie
Sasha
William

BLUE HEELER
Arnie
Bandit
Bow
Charlie
Daisy
Frank
Indie

Indy
Jake
Jessie
Jessy
Kate
Molly
Morgan
Pepper
Snitch
Suzy
Tex
Zac

BLUE HEELER
CROSS
Barra
Gus
Jesse
Kirra
Mardi
Matey
Millie
Patch
Sally
Tripe

BORDER COLLIE
Annie
Badger
Badgie
Badgy
Banjo
Barney
Baron
Beau
Bella
Belle
Ben

Bennie	Isabella	Pepper
Bentley	Jackson	Pete
Billie	Jake	Pippy
Billy	Jarra	Pogo
Bingo	Jed	Prince
Blake	Jedda	Puck
Bonnie	Jenna	River
Bonny	Jerry	Robbie
Bronwyn	Jess	Rosie
Bundy	Jessi	Rusky
Captain Jack	Jessica	Russel
Casper	Jessie	Sally
Ceiliddh	Jethro	Sam
Champ	Jordan	Samantha
Charlie	Kahli	Sandy
Chloe	Kama-Kazie	Sasha
Chrissy	Kim	Scuzzie
Chuffie	Kysha	Sharkie
Cinci	Lochley	Sheba
Coco	Lucy	Shelley
Codee	Maggie	Shelly
Dani	Maggie May	Sky
Digger	Max	Sooky
Dougal	Maxwell Smart	Sophie
Dylan	Miko	Swifty
Elvis	Misty	Tammie
Eros	Nappa	Tammy
Finn	Ned	Tasha
Flyte	Nellie	Tasman
Gabby	Nelly	Tia
Gemini	Otto	Tiffany
Gypsy	Paddy	Tiggy
Hamish	Panda	Tina
Harry	Pandy	Tincker
Heathcliffe	Patch	Toby
Holly	Pax	Tsar
Inca	Pearl	Tuskani
India	Peppa	Tyson

NAME YOUR PET!

Tyson Fluffy
Wally
Wrigley
Yo
Zac
Zack

BORDER COLLIE CROSS
Barney
Bear
Becky
Bella
Belle
Ben
Benji
Benny
Bert
Binger
Bingo
Binnie
Bob
Bonnie
Buck
Buffy
Bulldozer
Burnie

Buster
Butch
Buttons
Casey
Cassie
Champ
Charlie
Chloe
Cindy
Cleo
Coco
Conan
Ernie
Felix
Frankie
George
Gypsy
Hagar
Harley
Honey
Jade
Jake
Jaspa
Jed
Jesse
Jessie
Jinna
Kelly
Kiah
Kiki
Kosie
Lace
Lady
Louie
Micky
Mitsi
Mitzi
Negra

Nell
Nero
Nikki
Nipper
Ozzie
Pebbles
Penny
Ricky
Roxy
Sally
Sara
Scruff
Scruffy
Shandy
Sharna
Shedda
Skye
Sluggo
Sophie
Summer
Suske
Tess
Tillie
Tippy
Toovy
Vegemite
Waka
Whoopi
Winnie
Wolfie
Woofa
Zac
Zero
Ziggy
Zoe

BORDER TERRIER
Cinci

BORZOI
Misha
Nikki
Sascha
Toushka

BOSTON TERRIER
Fonz
Tasso

BOUVIER DES FLANDES
Tut

BOXER
Aggie
April
Archie
Argus
Beau
Beaujolais
Benson
Billie
Boogie
Boots
Boston
Briggs
Bronte
Busta
Buster
Butch
Cassie
Chet
Chrissy
Connie
County
Crystal
David

Dexter
Diva
Drummond
Ella
Ellie
Elly
Elsa
Flynn
Frankie
Ginny
Gunter
Hamish
Ike
Jack
Jake
Jemma
Jenny
Jessica
Jessie
Kadi
Kayla
Kelly
Kona
Kushka
Laddie
Lapsang
Leroy
Lulu
Mandy
Mick
Millie
Misty
O'hara
Oscar
Pepsi
Phoebe
Pripps
Red

Remy
Ruby
Sam
Scarlet
Scully
Sophie
Souchong
Spike
Stella
Takai
Tasha
Teresa
Tigga
Titan
Tyson
Winston
Yogi
Za Za
Zac

BOXER CROSS
Bonny
Buddy
Frankie
Hero
Jasmine
Jedda
Landi
Maggie
Niki
Rocky
Rosie
Sophie
Tasman

BRIARD
Bear
Bella

Michou
Sharna

BRITISH BULLDOG
Boston
Bronson
Cooleo
Fitty
Matey
Mildred
Pookie

BRITTANY SPANIEL
Blueberry
Kesh
Missy

BULL TERRIER
Beau
Ben
Blake
Bonny
Brutus
Bubbalouie
Chester
Cindy
Clara
Dexter
Emily
Fred
Harley
Hendrix
Jake
Jedda
Jessica
Jessie
K C

Kayler
Levi
Lucy
Maddy
Magpie
Mannie
Matilda
Max
Mindy
Noddy
O J
Otis
Rebel
Rex
Rhea
Risk
Rockie
Sam
Scamp
Sophie
Toro
Twiggy
Zack
Zodiac

BULL TERRIER CROSS
Anzac
Bandit
Ben
Benson
Bo
Bud
Bullie
Buster
Chilly
Commando
Connor

Cooper
Dorothy
Dr Spock
Eddie
Harley
Imogen
Jack
Jed
Joshua
Kelly
Lewis
Louis
Lucky
Lucy
Max
Misha
Mitchell
O.P
Oscar
Paw Paw
Psyche
Pugsly
Remi
Riggins
Rocco
Rocky
Roger
Sharne
Silver
Spider
Tex
Tinkerbell
Tojo
Tyson
Vamp

BULLMASTIFF
Benny

Jessie
Jolly
K C
Kelly
Lurar
Max
Ralph
Tyson

**BURNESE
MOUNTAIN DOG**
Elsa
Heidi
Tess

CAIRN TERRIER
Abbey
Amelia
Aussie
Bear
Bunty
Cas
Chloe
Coco
Cracker
Ginny
Holly
Jessie
Jesuis
Laddie
Lexie
Lottie
Milo
Minty
Mufty
Oscar
Puppy
Rory

Rupert
Sampson
Scruffy
Smudge
Splash
Tor
Toto
Whiskey

**CATTLE DOG
(STUMPY TAIL)**
Billie
Bindy
Clancy
Huey
Knuckles
Lucy
Ringo
Santa
Swiggles

**CATTLE DOG
CROSS**
Abby
Agnes
Agro
Angel
Angus
Beebes
Bella
Ben
Bernie
Bert
Bessie
Billie
Billy
Bimbo
Bluey

Bodhisattva
Bonnie
Bosley
Bouncer
Bowie
Bronco
Buck
Buddy
Bundy
Candy
Casey
Champ
Charlie
Cider
Clare
Coco
Conan
Daisy
Danny
Daphne
Darth
Di Di
Doogie
Douglas
Duke
Echo
Elsa
Fang
Fanta
Fudge
Gemma
Gipsy
Gladys
Goanna
Gosha
Guai
Gussie
Helmut

NAME YOUR PET!

Hendrix
Holly
Humphrey
Jack
Jake
Jasper
Jess
Jesse
Jessica
Jessie
Jet
Jim Beam
Jimmy
Judy
Karma
Kate
Kirra
Kong
Krusty
Lady
Link
Lucky
Lucy
Mac
Maddie
Maddy
Madgi
Mambo
Max
Maxie
Mickie

Midnight
Missy
Mogul
Montague
Muffin
Mungo
Muppy
Mustang
Narelle
Nugget
Oddie
Ozzie
Patch
Pepsi
Pip
Poochy
Pup
Rasta
Rastas
Red
Roman
Rory
Rosie
Rusty
Sake
Sally
Sandy
Scruffy
Scully
Shara
Sharni
Shelly
Smokey
Snoopy
Spike
Sqizzy
Sting
Stumpy

Tao
Tara
Tasha
Tess
Threebee
Tiger
Tilly
Tim
Tina
Tippie
Toby
Tosh
Trixie
Twit
Ty
Virginia
Waggles
Whiskey
Wilbur
Winnie
Womble
Zac
Zach
Ziggy
Zilla
Zoe

CAVALIER KING CHARLES CROSS
Jack
Patch
Sashie
Sos

CAVALIER KING CHARLES
Alice
Alicia

Aloysius
Badger
Bailey
Barney
Baxter
Beau
Beaumont
Bella
Ben
Bertie
Bo
Buddy
Buster
Casper
Cassie
Cassy
Charlie
Chipie
Chloe
Cindy
Cleo
Cody
Dani
Danny
Dimmy
Dougal
Dylan
Feliny
Fletcher
Fluffy
Footy
Gemma
Georgie
Groover
Henry
Hero
Holly
Honey

Indiana
Jamie
Jessica
Jessie
Jip
Katie
Kelley
Kyle
Leia
Lily
Lucy
Magnus
Marcus
Marty
Max
Mia
Milo
Minnie
Misty
Mitchell
Mr Tuppypuddle
Mufti
Murphy
Nellie
Niki
Nutmeg
Pepe
Phantom
Pixie
Polpi
Rex
Ricky
Risky
Robbie
Rocky
Rosa
Rosey
Rosie

Ruby
Ruffles
Rusty
Sally
Sam
Sandy
Scruffles
Scrumpy
Sebastian
Sophie
Spangles
Toby
Toff
Tommy
Toppa
Toto
Tuck
Wilbur
Winnie
Woodstock
Zac
Zack
Zippy

CENTRAL ASIAN SHEEPDOG
Hattab

CHIHUAHUA (LONG COAT)
Bonnie
Cleo
Clyde
Flufflett
Jazzmine
Jessie
Joshua
Mandy

NAME YOUR PET!

Minnie
Peppi
Sheba
Snowball
Susie
Tara
Tiffany
Toby

CHIHUAHUA (SMOOTH COAT)
Alex
Alice
Bambi
Benji
Billy
Brutus
Bully
Caesar
Charlie
Chester
Chiquita
Chloe
Dhugal
Dominic
Elle
Fifi
Fleur
Gi Gi
Gizmo
Honey
Jim
Joli
Lecie
Maddie
Matey
Milo
Miya

Muffin
Muffy
Muski
Nick
Nicki
Pancho
Percy
Pinnie
Pixie
Poppy
Rusty
Sashie
Shaz
Show Off
Shuftee
Snoopy
Sooty
Sophie
Spooky
Stella
Sunshine
Tango
Teddy
Teddy Bear
Tiko
Toby
Topsy
Whoopy
Zoe

CHIHUAHUA CROSS
Arthur
Bill
Chiko
Gizmo
Grungle
Hector
Junior

Marlene
Max
Mitch
Pancho
Popeye
Tarah
Tina
Wally

CHINESE CRESTED DOG
Leslie
Sophie

CHOW CHOW
Bear
Buffy
Chow
Choy
Chun
Fizz
Fluffy
Jade
Khan
Kimmi
Milly
Mishka
Puppy
Rupert
Winnie
Zebedee

COCKER SPANIEL
Adage
Amber
Amy
Ashley
Bagel

Barney	Hobo	Penny
Bella	Holly	Peppi
Ben	Honey	Pepsi
Bentleigh	Hugo	Pippi
Billy	Humphrey	Pokie
Blue	Indigo	Princess
Bobby	Isaac	Rambo
Bonnie	Isabella	Rastus
Bonny	Jake	Regan
Bruno	Jamey	Remington
Brutus	Jasper	Rocky
Buffy	Jedda	Ruffles
Bullet	Jess	Rusty
Bunty	Jody	Sally
Buster	Joey	Sam
Cassie	Jolly	Sandy
Charlie	Joshua	Scout
Chester	Lachlan	Sheba
Chimba	Lady	Skye
Chloe	Lance	Snoopy
Christie	Les	Sophie
Cindy	Lucy	Suzie
Digby	Lulu	Sweep
Digger	Mac	Tammy
Dizzy	Meg	Tasha
Duke	Melanie	Tessa
Emily	Merry	Tilly
Emma	Millie	Toby
Fred	Mindy	Topy
Fudge	Missie	Tuffy
Gemma	Monet	Wally
George	Monty	Zac
Georgie	Noddy	Ziggy
Goldie	Oliver	
Gus	Orpheus	**COCKER SPANIEL**
Gypsy	Oscar	**CROSS**
Harley	Patch	Bo
Harriet	Paula	Chloe

NAME YOUR PET!

Dave
Fifi
Inky
Max
Sunny
Tess
Thai
Tully

COLLIE (ROUGH)
Abby
Astro Boy
Ben
Blaze
Candy
Casey
Gaucho
Holly
Honey
Jaegar
Jake
Jessie
Lad
Laddie
Lassie
Maxwell
Melody
Monty
Oscar
Rebel
Sally
Sandy
Schatzie
Sheena
Sheltie
Sultan
Taja
Wally

COLLIE (SMOOTH)
Ashlea
Honey
Jasper
Leisha

COLLIE CROSS
Arnold
Babes
Badger
Bear
Beau
Bernard
Biffy
Bonnie
Bowie
Cassie
Clyde
David
Dorothy
Dusty
Elkie
Flossie
Foxie
Grumpy
Heidi
Honey
Jasmine
Jenny
Jinta
Josephine
Kali
Kim
Kinko
Kipper
Lady
Lorenzo
Lucky Dog

Max
Millie
Mischa
Moddy
Ned
Paddington
Patch
Puddie
Rusty
Samba
Sasha
Simba
Skamp
Sooty
Tammy
Teba
Teo Pepe
Tess
Tex
Vinnie-Sue

CORGI
Cracker
Heidi
Jill
Kitchener
Lassie
Maggie
Morgan
Paddy
Rexy
Robbo
Sam
Snooks
Stormy

CORGI CROSS
Bear

Beetle
Ben
Betty
Brandy
Chloe
Cleo
Dave
Felix
Fella
Ginger
Gussie
Honey
Jack
Mandy
Molly
Pixote
Ralph
Sally
Scamp
Scruffy
Shelley
Sophie
Sparkey
Stumpy
Tinny
Webster

**CURLEY COATED
RETRIEVER**
Chaz
Chilli
Harley

**DACHSHUND
(LONGHAIR)**
Ashanti
Beau
Bert

Bonny
Cilla
Clara
Fergie
Fritz
Jessief
Max
Polly
Sinbad

**DACHSHUND
(MINATURE
LONGHAIR)**
Bogart
Chico
Cleopatra
Emma
Lady
Lucy
Mack
Mischief
Tosh

**DACHSHUND
(MINI
SMOOTHHAIR)**
Annie
Bam-Bam
Caleb
Ceasar
Cilla
Cleo
Fritzy
Genie
George
Jessica
Murphy
Sally

Skip
Sylvester
Yani

**DACHSHUND
(SMOOTHHAIR)**
Alf
Basil
Beau
Bert
Charlie
Copper
Daisy
Duke
Harrison
Holly
King
Lilly
Lottie
Mandy
Milamber
Missy
Patsy
Pepper
Piccolo
Pickles
Rommel
Rudi
Sammy
Snags
Spice
Stubby
Sugar
Willy

**DACHSHUND
(WIREHAIR)**
Alf

NAME YOUR PET!

Leah
Mishy

**DACHSHUND
CROSS**
Bonnie
Doods
Dumpster
Fred
Gyp
Jasmine
Max
Mopsy
Morticia
Puddles
Sadie
Snoopy
Spanna
Tiger
Tinks

DALMATION
Abbey
Archer
Bazil
Beau
Bella
Bernie
Boris
Boss

Cara
Carla
Cila
Daisy
Didi
Ditto
Elliott
Finn
Freckles
Georgie
Gus
Gypsy
Huey
Isabel
Jaala
Jack Daniels
Jackson
Jessie
Jock
Kesha
Kouki
Leroy
Lucky
Lucy
Magic
Maverick
Max
Napoleon
Peaches
Pepa
Radar
Raffles
Sam
Sara
Snitzel
Spot
Tia
Tim

Tochka
Totchka
Trixie
Victor
Webster
Ziggy
Zippy
Zoe

**DALMATION
CROSS**
Billy
Gemma
Guzzi
Sam
Skip
Zac
Zebb

**DANDIE DINMONT
TERRIER**
Bonnie
Honey
Tinkerbell

DINGO CROSS
Ding
Ruff
Spencer

DOBERMAN
Adolph
Apollo
Bonnie
Bonny
Bronson
Cane
Chu

Claude
Coco
Cori
Dallas
Dog
Duke
Eva
George
Heidi
Jedda
Jess
Kirra
Kirri
Krug
Kuru
Lily
Mandy
Max
Mindy
Misha
Orrah
Pheobe
Rebel
Remington
Remo
Rex
Rocky
Sarah
Schultz
Shah
Sheba
Star
Tara
Tasha
Tequila
Tiger
Velvet
Zeus

DOBERMAN CROSS
Buster
Capri
Chester
Doba
Elle
Emma
Gus
Lola
Luke
Max
Megs
Portia
Raff
Sam
Sarah
Sascha
Sasha
Scoobie
Sophie
Spot
Stregga
Tequila
Tyson
Yoda

ELKHOUND
Loupo
Sid

ENGLISH POINTER
Saas

ENGLISH SETTER
Byron
Daisy
Holly
Honey

Jilly
Lindy Lou
Rosie
Sally

ENGLISH SPRINGER
Cherran
Chip
Flloyd
Ginny
Kaydee
Portia
Ruby

FOX TERRIER
Beefer
Ben
Bill
Brandy
Chelsea
Cindy
Claudia
Desko
Foxy
Guinness
Jai
Jenken
Jenny
Lettie
Max
Molly
Ooshi
Oscar
Peggy
Pip
Pixie
Princess

NAME YOUR PET!

Pretty
Rex
Sabbie
Samuel
Sheba
Slam
Spud
Star
Toby
Tootsie
Trixie
Wally

FOX TERRIER
(WIREHAIR)
Barney
Foxie
Garrick
Lottie
Misty
Rosie
Winnie

FOX TERRIER
CROSS
Axel
Barney
Bessie
Bindy
Bulla
D J
Elley
Harley
Huey
Jack
Jake
Lady Effi
Lily

Millie
Missy
Molly
Monty
Nala
Noddy
Quizzy
Ralf
Ralph
Sally
Sam
Scruffy
Sindy
Snoopy
Snowy
Sooty
Speck
Spike
Suzie
Tasha
Taylor
Tin Tin
Willy

FOX TERRIER
MINATURE
April
Binny
Blackie
Bonny
Bubba
Buster
Carmen
Cassegrain
Cindy
Cleo
Cloe
Corky

Danny
Dinkie
Doris
Foxy
Frankie
Jazz
Lady
Leo
Lil
Maddison
Maisie
Matches
Matic
Max
Mikey
Nip
Oscar
Patch
Peter
Pippa
Robbie
Rox
Rudik
Sally
Simpson
Sophie
Spot
Stumpy
Sugsy
Sweety
Titch

Trixie

FOXHOUND
Rex

GERMAN
SHEPHERD DOG
Amber
Apache
Arnie
Arno
Attila
Ausie
Aussie
B J
Baci
Bandit
Bando
Basil
Bear
Bella
Ben
Biatta
Bindi
Blackie
Blaza
Blitz
Bo
Bodie
Bonnie
Boris
Boss
Bosun
Brando
Braveheart
Brewster
Bronson
Brooklyn

Brutus
Buggs
Buster
Butch
Caesar
Carla
Casey
Cassandra
Cassey
Cassie
Castor
Cerberus
Charley
Charlotte
Chato
Chelsea
Chester
Chloe
Cindy
Clare
Claude
Clea
Coco
Cody
Columbus
Con
Dash
Deputy
Des
Dudley
Elka
Elsa
Emma
Feather
Flash
Fletch
Floppy
Fookchai

Frankie
Freya
Frida
Frieda
Fripon
Gemini
Georgia
Gina
Goliath
Gorggy
Greta
Gypsy
Hannah
Happy
Heckle
Heidi
Hektor
Helga
Henry
Holly
Honey
Hugo
Ilka
Jaga
Jai
Jake
Jasmine
Jasper
Jazz
Jeckle
Jedda
Jerry
Jess
Jessie
Jessy
Jett
Jezabel
Jimmy

NAME YOUR PET!

Jo Jo	Maverick	Rommel
Josie	Max	Rose
Kahli	Mayhem	Rowdy
Kahn	Melody	Ruby
Kai	Merlin	Rupert
Kaiser	Mischa	Rusty
Kala	Misho	Sable
Kali	Missy	Sally
Karl	Misty	Sam
Karla	Monty	Samber
Kashi	Moon	Sampson
Kato	Napolean	Sanburg
Kelly	Natasha	Sara
Ken	Negus	Sasha
Khan	Nicki	Schatze
Khia	Nikita	Sebastian
Kiara	Nina	Shad
Kiera	Nitro	Shadow
Kim	Noni	Sharna
Kimba	Nushka	Sheba
Kola	Odessa	Sheema
Kosmo	Olympic	Shep
Kubilai	Otto	Sherman
Kublai	Peppi	Shika
Kzar	Pete	Skye
Laddie	Pollux	Spunt
Leo	Puddles	Stella
Lionel	Puppy	Stoonce
Lisa	Ralph	Storm
Luke	Rambo	Sultan
Lupo	Rani	Sunny
Luther	Raphie	Taipan
Mac	Rebel	Tammy
Maim	Red	Tara
Marla	Rex	Tasha
Marshall	Robert	Teemie
Mask	Rocky	Tess
Matey	Rolf	Tessa

88

Ti
Toby
Togo
Tonto
Trio
Tugbah
Twinkle
Twisty
Tyrone
Tyson
Vooki
Webster
Willy
Windy
Wolf
Woof
Yindi
Zaar
Zac
Zachery
Zaras
Zeus
Zoe
Zola
Zoul
Zulu

**GERMAN
SHEPHERD CROSS**
Akela
Alexander
Anna
Anzac
Apostrophe
Aurora
Barnes
Basil
Bear

Beau
Bert
Billy
Binkie
Blackie
Bogart
Boof
Brogie
Bugsy
Buldy
Buster
Byron
Callan
Casey
Charlie
Chloe
Churchill
Cindy
Cleo
Clint
Coco
Conan
Cosmo
Cyrus
Dak
Deputy
Diesel
Dino
Ekke
Emma
Eva
Floyd
Foxy
Goldie
Gus
Hamlet
Harley
Harry

Holly
Hooch
Jack
Jackie
Jackson
Jake
Jasmine
Jasper
Jemma
Jess
Jessie
Jimmy
Karl
Karla
Kelly
Kenzie
King
Kiri
Kiwi
Kiya
Lacey
Lady
Lice
Lucky
Lucy
Ma
Max
Mayhem
Mickey
Mickie
Milly
Mischa
Mish
Mitch
Mitsi
Molly
Monty
Nacyre

Nugget
Oliver
Oscar
Otis
Polly
Puppy
Ralph
Rani
Rastas
Rebel
Reg
Rocky
Roxy
Rusty
Sabre
Sally
Sam
Sandy
Sasha
Sebastian
Seoul
Sharna
Shayne
Sheba
Shelly
Shitan
Skipper
Sky
Skye
Smarty
Sonic
Sonny
Sooty
Sultan
Sundane
Tabu
Tara
Tarson

Tessa
Thunder
Tia
Tico
Tinley
Tisha
Tobi
Toby
Tor
Trudie
Wanda
Wesley
Windy
Wolf
Wolfgang
Yeni
Zac
Ziggy
Zoe
Zolly

**GERMAN
SHORTHAIRED
POINTER**
Arnie
Belay
Ben
Bruno
Bundy
Buzzy
Collette
Cyrus
Deco
Doris
Duchess
Else
Harold
Heidi

Jaffa
Jessie
Katerina
Martha
Maude
Melodie
Monty
Nooee
Oscar
Polly
Pritzy
Rex
Ridge
Sam
Schultz
Shadow
Shona
Sucher
Taj
Treble
Zac
Zahn
Zippy

**GERMAN
SHORTHAIRED
POINTER CROSS**
Charlie
Djawi
Kaiser

**GLEN OF IMMAAL
TERRIER**
Arnold

**GOLDEN
RETRIEVER**
Adrian

Alaska	Byron	Gus
Alex	Caesar	Hamish
Amber	Carby	Happi
Angel	Cassie	Harry
Apollo	Chanel	Harry
Arthur	Charlie	Henry
Aurora	Chauncey	Hugo
B.B	Chester	Huntly
Banjo	Chip	Jake
Barney	Chipper	James
Bart	Chloe	Jasper
Bass	Clara	Jedda
Beau	Coach	Jessica
Bella	Coke	Jessie
Benji	Coral	Kane
Benny	Cruise	Katie
Benson	Daisy	Keats
Bess	Danny	Kellie
Betsy	Deefa	Keppe
Bonnie	Dexter	Kheva
Bonny	Diesel	Killa
Boris	Dixie	Kori
Boston	Dolche	Kyle
Bozo	Doolan	Lady
Brandy	Dusty	Laika
Brett	Ella	Laxy
Bridget	Ellie	Leroy
Brodie	Elsie	Libby
Bronte	Emma	Lincoln
Buddy	Ernest	Lucia
	Fergie	Lucy
	Folly	Maddie
	Fred	Marcus
	Frodo	Max
	Gemma	Maxwell
	Gera	Meg
	Gertrude	Michael
	Goldie	Millie
		Mogus

NAME YOUR PET!

Mojo
Molly
Monty
Nugget
Oliver
Oscar
Petra
Polly
Pollyanna
Puddy
Rachael
Raj
Ralph
Raphael
Rasmus
Rebel
Red
Reggie
Rhett
Richmond
Rocky
Ronnie
Rosie
Rufus
Rupert
Saffran
Sally
Sam
Samba
Sandy
Sasha
Saxon
Sebastian
Shane
Shea
Sheba
Sherrie
Shona Mercy

Skipper
Skye
Smokey
Spencer
Suzy
Tailor
Teddy
Tess
Tessa
Toby
Trudy
Truffles
Viking
Wendell
Windsor
Winnie
Yamba
Zac
Zachary
Zara
Ziggy

GOLDEN RETRIEVER CROSS
Buffy
Bunker
Charlie
Elliot
Jess
Keesha
Lassie
Nellie
Pup
Puppy
Rolly
Sam
Sasha
Scally

Spot

GORDON SETTER
Alex
Guinness
Jake
Mark Twain
Sunsie

GREAT DANE
Ace
Adeva
Arnie
Banjo
Bloss
Bonny
Chester
Dawn
Harley
Jemma
Jess
Klepsie
Mungo
Nicky
Phoneix
Shergon
Texas
Zoe

GREAT DANE CROSS
Bear
Maxine
Moet
Tasha

GREYHOUND
Ashley

Baby
Best Pal
Jessie
Ringo
Shampers
Silva

**GRIFFON
BRUXELLOIS**
Brutus
Griff

**HAMILTON-
STOVARE**
Nibbles

HUNGARIAN PULI
Bogi
Buksi
Cuki

**HUNGARIAN
VIZSLA**
Bella
Enya
Helga
Oscar

HUSKY CROSS
Max

IRISH SETTER
Jedda
Kerry
Milly
Monoch
Shamrock

IRISH TERRIER
Tara

IRISH WOLFHOUND
Arnie
Killarney
Romulous
Sara
Sebastian

**IRISH WOLFHOUND
CROSS**
Boshka

**ITALIAN
GREYHOUND**
Luke

**JACK RUSSELL
CROSS**
Athena
Brutus
Buffy
Candy
Gilla
Herbie
Hercules
Jessie

Max
Peppy

**JACK RUSSELL
TERRIER**
Blocka
Bobbie
Buster
Cammie
Chad
Clover
Daisy
Dan
Doug
Eddie
Elle
Elmo
Fred
Gila
Hamish
Harold
Henry
Holly
Hurley
Jack
Jackie
Jackson
Jake
Jasper
Jessie
Jimmy
Keeper
Larrikin
Levi
Louise
Lucy
Max
Milo

NAME YOUR PET!

Mindy
Missy
Nimm
Nina
Nugget
Otto
Paddy
Patch
Peggy
Penny
Phoebe
Pippa
Ralph
Russell
Sasha
Shadow
Sharky
Snoopy
Snowy
Stolli
Tayla
Ted
Tess
Tessa
Thelma
Tiny
Tyrrells
Victor
Wally
Zoe

**JAPANESE CHIN
CROSS**
Biggles

KARABASH
Minnie

KEESHOND
Akeisha
Bear
Buffy
Charlie
Codie
Jessie
Kristie
Lucy
Marley
Mickey
Mischief
Mishka
Muffy
Nicholas
Nuff
Peppi
Tiger
Tollana

KELPIE CROSS
Tilly
Allie
Andy
Annabelle
Ashe
Babs
Basil
Bayette
Bear
Beau
Bella
Bess
Bessy
Betty
Biggles
Billie
Billy

Bindi
Black Devil
Blackie
Blondy
Bo
Bob
Bodie
Bonnie
Bonny
Boris
Brandy
Bronson
Bud
Bullett
Bundy
Bungy
Cam
Candy
Cane
Cara
Carly
Casey
Cassie
Cassy
Charlie
Charlie Brown
Checker
Chippie
Chisel
Cleo
Comet
Constanza
Cosmo
Digger
Dolly
Dusty
Ebony
Eccles

Elle
Emma
Fletcher
Franky
Freckles
Freebee
Fuschia
Gemma
Gina
Ginger
Gordon
Greenie
Grub
Guinea
Gus
Gypsy
Harley
Heathie
Heidi
Honey
Husha
Hutch
India
Irish
Isobella
Jack
Jackie
Jake
Jasper
Jed
Jedda
Jess
Jessie
Jet
Jo
Joe
Jones
Julian

Junior
Kaos
Kelly
Kenny
Kesh
Kim
Kirra
Kossa
Kyah
Lady
Lenny
Leroy
Lewis
Licorice
Lilly
Liquorice
Little Boy
Lizzy
Lucy
Luka
Maddie
Made
Madi
Mavis
Max
Mickey
Milo
Mindy
Missy
Mitzi
Molly
Monty
Myra
Nacyre
Nala
Nancy
Nero
Nosey

Oggy
Opal
Opit
Otis
Paddie
Patches
Pav
Peppie
Pibba
Pippy
Poppy
Porridge
Puddles
Puppy
Quattro
Ralph
Raphael
Razz
Rocky
Rommel
Rummy
Rusty
Sabie
Sam
Sasha
Scamp
Shadow
Shandy
Sheba
Sid
Skye
Snapper
Sniffy
Socks
Sophie
Spanner
Spike
Squeak

Stan	Zac	Barney
Star	Zach	Bart
Stiv	Zena	Bea
Susie	Zimi	Beasley
Suzy	Zoe	Beau
Systar	Zox	Bella
Taja	Zulu	Ben
Tania		Benji
Ted	**KERRY BLUE**	Bess
Tess	**TERRIER**	Blossom
Tessa	Abby	Bobby
Tessy		Bonny
Thai	**KERRY BLUE**	Boots
Thom	**TERRIER CROSS**	Brandy
Tiger	Harry	Buster
Tigger		Chester
Tiny	**KING CHARLES**	Clancy
Tippy	**SPANIEL**	Cleo
Tipsy	Buttons	Coke
Tommy	Charlie	Daisy
Trev	Hamish	Dino
Tyrone	Jaspa	Doris
Tyson	Jasper	Douglas
Vegemite	Joshua	Dreva
Walter	Lady	Duke
Whitney	Morrison	Dusky
Winkie	Polly	Ebony
Woolly	Wickerty Wack	Ella
Wozzie	Zac	Eppie
		Floozy
	LABRADOR	George
	Abigail	Goldie
	Alexander	Gordon
	Amber	Hannah
	Andy	Harry
	Angus	Hugo
	Archibald	Huxley
	Astro	Jackson

Jake	Ollie	**LABRADOR CROSS**
Jashu	Oscar	Alice
Jasmin	Petal	Angus
Jasper	Poochy	Arrow
Jed	Prince	Augustus
Jerry	Raphael	Axl
Jess	Rex	Bags
Jessica	Ricky	Barney
Jet	Rocket	Beau
Jim	Rocky	Bella
Jordie	Roland	Ben
Joshua	Rum	Billy
Kelly	Sam	Blackett
Kim	Samantha	Blackie
Kimba	Samson	Blanco
Larry	Sandy	Bogart
Leo	Sasha	Bon Bon
Lindy	Sausage	Boris
Lizzie	Shaq	Brady
Louis	Shauna	Brindle
Lucky	Sheba	Brodie
Lucy	Snowy	Buggy
Mac	Sooty	Buster
Madison	Sophie	Butch
Matilda	Sunny	Calvin
Max	Sunshine	Cassie
Maxi	Tarra	Cato
Miffy	Tessa	Chelsea
Millie	Toby	Chenoa
Mishka	Topaz	Chicho
Mocha	Tyson	Chloe
Molly	Victoria	Chrissie
Monty	Winston	Chrissy
Murphy	Wombi	Cindy
Natasha	Woody	Cleo
Nelson	Zac	Cliff
Noodles	Zoe	Dana
Oakleigh	Zudnik	Didi

NAME YOUR PET!

Ellie	Lady	Rusty
Elsa	Lenny	Sail
Fonzarelli	Louise	Sally
Fred	Lucy	Sam
Gaby	Maddy	Samantha
Gemma	Mary	Sambucca
George	Maverick	Sandy
Georgie	Max	Sarai
Gerry	Minx	Sasha
Gogo	Missy	Sasky
Goldea	Mogs	Sebastian
Gordon	Molly	Sebby
Grimsley	Muggsy	Shandy
Happy	Nelson	Simba
Hashish	Nicky	Sooty
Heidi	Ninja	Sophie
Henry	Oliver	Stumpy
Hobbs	Oscar	Syd
Honey	Paddy	T C
Honto	Peggy	Tammy
Hope	Pippy	Tarra
Indy	Polly	Terror
Jack	Poochie	Tess
Jacob	Pouncer	Thug
Jamie Lee	Power	Tia
Jasmine	Pup	Tigger
Jasper	Purdey	Tim
Jayjay	Rags	Tippy
Jedda	Ralph	Tish
Jesper	Rambo	Toby
Jessica	Rayna	Velvet
Jimah	Repo	Yan
Jody	Rex	Zane
Josh	Rina	Zara
Kali	Ringo	Zedd
Katy	Roger	Zilla
Kelly	Rosie	Zoe
Krusty	Roup	Zorro

LAKELAND
TERRIER
Harriet
Tuffy

LHASA APSO
Beau
Bundy
Fang
Frederick
Fudge
Gizmo
Honey
Jessie
Khan
Lucy
Merlin
Michelle
Midget
Mitzi
Mitzy
Ollie
Panda
Runah
Sasha
Schnook
Sharday
Shoupay
Simba

Tom
Tuk Tuk
Walter

LHASA APSO
CROSS
Bismark
Freeway
Oocky

LOWCHEN
Arko
Kim
Leo
Puppy
Romeo
Villian

MALTESE
Angel
Angus
Annabell
Astro
Beau
Bella
Ben
Benji
Beppu
Bianca
Billy
Bingo
Blossom
Bo
Bob
Bobby
Bonnie
Boss
Boz

Brut
Bunty
Byron
Candy
Casper
Cassie
Chanel
Chanti
Charles
Charlie
Chelsea
Chi-Chi
Chloe
Clare
Claude
Coco
Cosmo
Cuddles
Damien
Dan
Dexter
Dougal
Electra
Elemer
Eli
Elle
Ellie
Emma
Errol
Georgie
Henry
Holly
Huggy
Jake
Jasmine
Jay
Jay Jay
J D

NAME YOUR PET!

Jemma
Jessie
Kazna
Kip
Laddie
Leo
Lucky
Lucy
Lulu
Lyndy
Manoulis
Matilda
Max
Millie
Milly
Mindy
Minte
Minty
Missy
Mitzi
Mitzy
Molly
Mopsy
Muffin
Muffy
Mungichi
Nellie
Nicky
Nina
Olive
Oscar
Pebbles
Penbeh
Penny
Peta
Philbert
Phoebe
Pipi

Popcorn
Popeye
Popsy
Princess
Pup
Ragamuffin
Rambo
Robert
Rocky
Rusty
Sam
Samson
Sandy
Sasha
Scottie
Scruffy
Shadow
Shandy
Sir William
Snoopy
Snow
Snowy
Sophie
Spike
Sprocket
Stud
Susie
Sydney
Tammy
Teddy
Tess
Tessa
Tiffany
Timmy
Tinkerbell
Toby
Tom
Tootsie

Tuggles
Tyler
Tyson
Whiskey
William
Winnie
Winston
Yasmine
Zac
Ziggy

MALTESE CROSS

Abbie
Angus
Archie
Baffi
Bazzle
Bella
Bilson
Bindy
Bobbie
Bonnie
Bonny
Boofy
Boumba
Bruno
Buffy
Busby
Casper
Chamois
Chippie
Chloe
Chrissy
Coco
Cuddles
Daisy
D J
Dusty

Eddie
Ella
Eva
Flintstone
Floss
Geofrey
Geordie
Gina
Hamish
Harley
Holly
Iggy
Jack
Jade
Jamey
Jefferson
Jessie
Kahlua
Kara
Katie
Kazna
Kobi
Koukla
Latte
Loo
Lucy
Manulis
Mattie
Minny
Mishy
Moo Moo
Mr Fudge
Muffy
Pansy
Pepper
Peppi
Peppy
Pipp

Pixie
Pom Pom
Rosie
Rosy
Saffy
Sam
Sandy
Sasha
Scruffie
Scruffy
Shakespeare
Snowflake
Star
Suscha
Taka
Tiffany
Tiggy
Timmy
Toby
Vesla
Zac
Ziggy

MANCHESTER TERRIER
Bonnie
Prim

MAREMMA SHEEPDOG
Micka
Mastiff
Basil
Zugli

MINIATURE FOX TERRIER
Amy

Beau
Hannibal
Harry
Lady
Leah
Max
Oscar
Pixie
Popcorn
Winnie

MINIATURE PINSCHER
Budget
Tootsie

NEWFOUNDLAND
Angus
Baby
Gypsy
Holly
Morse
Nanny
Rocky
Skoshi

NEWFOUNDLAND CROSS
Clyde
Jessie

NORWICH TERRIER
Skipper

OLD ENGLISH SHEEPDOG
Bear
Binkey

101

Boofy
Byron
Emma
Floyd
Georgie
Jasmine
Kate
Ling Ling
Matilda
Missy
Pazazz
Samantha
Scamp
Teddy
Tootie Fruity

PAPILLON
Bachi
Kasey
Kelly
Monty
Percy
Pixie
Pluto
Silvey

PEKINGESE
Choo Choo
Chou Chou
Jo Jo
Ming
Oscar
Ricky
Susy
Tarka-Tu
Toy
Trixie
Winnie

PEMBROKE CORGI
Dylan
Emma
Molly
Oliver
Robbie
Snuffles
Windsor

PIT BULL TERRIER
Assasin
Bronson
Captain
Grizzly
Lady
Rana
Zen

POINTER
Harley
Rambo

POINTER CROSS
Max

POMERANIAN
Beau
Billy
Brandy
Doo Doo
Flossy
Gizmo
Lara
Rusty
Shari
Shy
Sooty
Sydney

Tamsin
Ted
Topuli
Truffles
Twopence
Ziggy

POMERANIAN CROSS
Boney
Buffy
Jessie
Lucky
Puppy
Sherona
Tia
Trent

POODLE (MINIATURE)
Albert
Alexis
Alfred
Amanda
Amber
Andy
Annabel
Babette
Banjo
Bankus
Basil
Bazzie
Bear
Beau
Beaubeau
Bella
Ben
Berri

Billy
Bo
Bobbie
Bobby
Bolly
Bonnie
Brandy
Bubble
Buttons
Byron
Cameo
Candy
Cara
Charlie
Cherie
Chloe
Ciggi
Cindy
Claude
Coco
Couter
Ebony
Eleanore
Fee
Felix
Fifi
Fluffy
Fred
Freddy
Gemma
Georgie
Gigi
Goldie Ponx
Gus
Gyzmo
Harriet
Harry
Heidi

Henry
Hermie
Holly
Inky
Jackson
Jaffa
Jedda
Jemma
Jet
Jicky
Josie
Kali
Kimba
Kizzy
Laura
Lily
Louie
Louis
Lu Lu
Lucy
Mabo
Matt
Max
Meesha
Mikey
Mimi
Misty
Mitzie
Moet
Montgomery
Monty
Muffin
Nancy
Navarro
Nicholas
Niki
Nipper
Noodle

Ollie
Oscar
Paw Paw
Peggy Sue
Penny
Pepe
Peppa
Peppi
Pierre
Pola
Pompei
Pumpkin
Ralph
Roli
Rudi
Russell
Sadie
Sally
Sam
Scamp
Sebastion
Sherry
Sooty
Suie
Susie
Syd
Sydney
Timothy
Toby

NAME YOUR PET!

Tom
Tosh
Tous
Tristram
Tyson
Vitto
Winnie
Winston
Zac
Ziggy
Zoe

POODLE (STANDARD)
Amy
Baci
Bruno
Cedric
Cluny
Coco
Elle
Fifi
Figaro
George
Georgie Girl
Jesse
Levi
Louis
Martine
Nicholas
Oscar
Phibi
Princess
Rachael
Rebel
Sasha
Sooty
Sophie

Tammy
Tiffany
Tori
Tyson
Zoe

POODLE (TOY)
Alexa
Archie
Banjo
Beau
Big Boy
Billie
Blossom
Brandy
Caniche
Cash
Charlie
Chloe
Chopin
Chrissy
Coco
Coco Channel
Coquette
Coquin
Corky
Cupid
Dan
Dolly
Ebony
Ella
Fergus
Genie
Gi Gi
Gilbey
Goldie
Grimmy
Jade

Jaffa
Jimmy
Kama
Kimba
Koyinu
Leroy
Loretta
Lou Lou
Lucky
Luigi
Max
Mia
Mimi
Mimmy
Minta
Missy
Misty
Monique
Monte
Monty
Nancy
Nicky
Paddington
Pepe
Peppi
Pepsi
Perrier
Pierre
Pippin
Rambo
Rani
Rascal
Rohnda
Roisin
Rolly
Sacha
Soda
Sooty

Sophie
Suga
Thomas
Tia
Tootsie
Trigger
Tuppence
Walter
Wilfred
Willie
Yves
Zoe

POODLE CROSS
Alexis
Bubbles
Bucky
Char Bon
Charlie
Chloe
Coco
Comet
Curley
Gypsy
Hamish
Holly
Jasper
Jesse
Jessie
Jimmy
Jina
Mango
Marcus
Mctavish
Pippa
Polly
Rags
Ricky

Rommy
Rusty
Sally
Sam
Scamp
Storm
Tammy
Zap
Ziggy
Pug
Bilbo
Bongo
China
Chuzz
Dilly
Ebony
Hannibal
Harley
Harry
Jake
Jily
Katie
Minnie
Opal
Pixie
Pug
Pugsley
Rocket
Sebastian
Thomas
Tom
Winnie
Winston

PYRENEAN
MOUNTAIN DOG
Godzilla
Marquise

Ravel

RHODESIAN
RIDGEBACK
Barney
Ben
Bikita
Billy
Bronte
Brutus
Cassie
Charlie
Clyde
Daji
Deacon
D J
Dozer
Gidgit
Gypsy
Holly
Indiana
Java
Jenny
Jess
Jessie
Kenya
Kenza
Kimba
Leo
Leroy
Llhana
Mannie
Max
Mbili
Mischa
O J
Ra
Rafiki

NAME YOUR PET!

Rhumer
Rojo
Roxy
Shaka
Sheba
Simba
Sirius
Sophie
Spike
Sukey
Sybil
Tess
Willie
Xena
Zim

RIDGEBACK CROSS
Barnie
Beau
Chloe
Delila
Diesel
Ella
George
Holly
Honey
Jackson
Jaffa
Jake
Jessie
Jordy
Marlowe
Mayo
Megan
Mishka
Monte
Nugget

Rambo
Rocky
Ruby
Rusty
Safron
Simba
Spencer
Strauss
Trixie
Two
Vienna
Voodoo
Zach

ROTTWEILER
Alice
Amber
Arnie
Axel
Bambi
Baron
Barrumundi
Bear
Beau
Ben
Benson
Bill
Billy
Bismark
Blocker
Bollinger
Bonnie
Boof
Boss
Boston
Bronson
Brontie
Buffy

Caesar
Chelsea
Clarence
Claudie
Cloe
Conan
Daisy
Devil
Dodger
Doug
Dude
Dylan
Elle
Flint
Floyd
Fritz
Gypsy
Heidi
Herman
Iq
Jack
Jackson
Jake
Jasmine
Jemma
Jess
Jessie
Joshua
Kaiser
Karbon
Kaya
Kee
Kirby
Kong
Lou Lou
Lucy
Luke
Lulu

Magnum
Max
Maxine
Mischa
Molson
Monster
Murray
Nero
Ocker
Oke
Oscar
Panza
Pluto
Poppy
Ralph
Rana
Rocky
Rocky
Rochland
Ruby
Sabre
Sally
Sam
Samantha
Sasha
Shadow
Shamus
Shari
Shyra
Snake
Tatunka
Tazzie
Tess
Titus
Toby
Tom
Tyson
Tzar

Winston
Zac
Zaniel
Zara
Zeus
Zodiac
Zoe

ROTTWEILER CROSS
Ahara
Benson
Bimbo
Bingo
Boadicea
Bobby
Bonnie
Bora
Boris
Bronson
Bundy
Cleo
Deisel
Duke
Dutch
Grace
Helga
Jedda
Jess
Jessie
Jet
Kaos
Kiah
Kiera
Lucy
Max
Mia
Oke

Peace
Pepper
Puppy
Radar
Rocky
Rox
Roxanne
Roxy
Samantha
Shay
Simba
Snapper
Sponge
Tess
Titan
Whiskey

SAINT BERNARD
Abbe
Bundy
Leloy
Shoomba
Spot

SALUKI
Ky
Zebediah

SAMOYED
Bella

107

NAME YOUR PET!

Boris
Charlotte
Cuma
Diamond
Floyd
Geena
Holly
Jasper
Maverick
Meg
Misty
Natasha
Nellie
Nikita
Saravich
Sasha
Sha
Shandie
Sidney
Snowy
Syska
Tara
Zac

SCHNAUZER (GIANT)
Luke
Otis

SCHNAUZER (MINITURE)
Albert
Alice
Arly
Arnold
Beebee
Benny
Benson

Billy
Borris
Buster
Cara
Chevy
Claudia
Daisy
Dusty
Ellie
Emma
Georgie
Gilda
Halley
Harry
Heidi
Henry
Jessie
Jock
Joel
Johnnie
Leo
Lilly
Lizzy
Lucy
Martin
Matilda
Max
Misty
Monty
Nikki
Oliver
Oscar
Oskar
Otto
Panzer
Pepper
Pfeffer
Raffles

Reece
Remmy
Rolfe
Sally
Seana
Sky Rocket
Sofie
Stanzi
Steffi
Suki
Tess
Tiffany
Tootsie
Tuki
Waggs
Willy
Zac
Ziggy

SCHNAUZER (STANDARD)
Berlin
Bucky
Caro
Fella
Hannah
Harriette
Heidi
Helmut
Kaiser
Mischa
Panza
Patch
Petra
Rani
Sam
Sigmund
  Freud

Soxy
Willy
Zeus
Zoe

SCHNAUZER
CROSS
Charbon
Jack
Peekay
Shandy

SCOTTISH
TERRIER
Angus
Bess
Bonnie
Clyde
Dougal
Emily
Emma
Fred
Harley
Jasper
Jemma
Mactavish
Matilda
Mcdougall
Peggy-Sue
Pippa
Rose
Scottie Dog
Tilly
Tuppence

SCOTTISH
TERRIER CROSS
Ralph

SEALYHAM
TERRIER
Tammy

SHAR PEI
Busta
Sandy

SHEEP DOG
CROSS
Kimba
Mozart
Ramah

SHELTIE
Bonnie
Brandy
Alexander
Brigitte
Brook
Chelsea
Edwina
Fifi
Jack
Jock
Kaspar
Lochinvar
Lucy
Max
Maxwell
Miffy
Milou
Pebbles
Sheena
Tamea
Tammy
Tiger
Toffee

Tom
Zig Zag

SHETLAND
SHEEPDOG
Abbie
Bessie
Blossom
Charlie
Fhane
Harmony
Heather
Holly
Jester
Kate
Miffy
Perrie
Polo
R2
Radcliff
Sheena
Shelley
Skye
Tabitha
Tina
Trixie
Waldo

SHIH TZU
Ashley
Beau
Becky
Benson
Bobbie
Bogart
Bonnie
Boz
Bronte

NAME YOUR PET!

Chan
Charlie
Charlotte
Chelsea
Chessie
China
Chow Chow
Cleo
Dixie
Dominic
Dudley
Enya
Fran
Gismo
Gizmo
Harrison
Henry
Jasmine
Kasper
Katie
Lucy
Mambo
Max
Midget
Ming
Mischa
Missy
Misty
Mitsy

Molly
Morgan
Oscar
Ping
Poker
Scaggs
Scruffy
Shimi
Sky
Sparky
Spud
Sushi
Tashi
Ti
Tiger
Tina Mia
Tonkin
Tootsie
Topaz
Woky
Yoko
Yum Yum
Zig
Zita

SIBERIAN HUSKY
Bob
Bosco
Hobo
Jack
Jake
Nikita
Puppy
Queensky
Renegade
Sampson
Sebastian
Sequoia

Silver
Snowy
Storm
Tonka
Topsky
Zoe

SKYE TERRIER
Crumpet
Hamish
Skye

SPANIEL
Deli
Goldie
Rogue

SPRINGER
SPANIEL
Adelaide
Amber
Basil
Bess
Cathy
Chester
Daniel
Harlequin
Hugo
Kitt
Lucky
Max
Millie
Molly
Pippa
Polly
Rufus
Sam
Springer

Star
Tammy
Winnie

**STAFFORDSHIRE
BULL TERRIER**
Albert
Amber
Ampy
Annabel
Arnie
Ayla
Bali
Banjo
Basil
Bella
Bronson
Bruno
Buddy
Butch
Butts
Callan
Cassie
Ceasar
Chelsea
Brown
Chester
Cid
Cleveland
Coogee
Diamond
Dude
Dylan
Ellie
Ember
Fergus
Harley
Hattie

Heidi
Honey
Jake
Jazz
Jazzie
Jemma
Jess
Jessica
Jessie
Kahli
Karnie
Kate
Kayla
Kelly
Kenya
Kiwi
Kostya
Little One
Lucy
Maddy
Maggie
Max
Maxie
Minder
Molly
Monte
Nandi
Nessie
Nutmeg
Ollie
Pearle
Pie
Puppy
Ralph
Ren
Ridge
Roxy
Ruby

Sam
Shadow
Sid
Southern
Tao
Tara
Tess
Thor
Tiger
Tyson
William
Xerxes
Zac
Zulu

**STAFFORDSHIRE
CROSS**
Barney
Bess
Boston
Buster
Casey
Chi
Chloe
Chuck
Cody
Daisy
Deva
Duke
George
Goloum
Hooch
Indy
Ishka
Jade
Jedda
Jessie
Jordie

NAME YOUR PET!

Juno
Kane
Mac
Maggie
Mali
Missy
O J
Opal
Perro
Pucci
Rahm
Razzie
Rufus
Rusty
Sam
Sandy
Sheba
Siva
Tayo
Texan
Toby
Tyson
Wolfgang

SWEDISH
VALLHUND
Brook

SYDNEY TERRIER
Bubbles
Humphrey
Micky
Tammy
Tyson

TERRIER CROSS
Annabelle
Basil

Beau
Becky
Belle
Benji
Billy
Blue
Bonny
Bouncer
Brandy
Brooky
Bros
Brutus
Buddy
Buffy
Charlie
Chloe
Cindy
Cobber
Domino
Dotty
Fred
Harley
Harry
Holly
Honey
Hugh
Humphrey
Jack
Jacko
Jessie
Jethro
Jonty
Josie
King
Leroy
Lucy
Lucy Brown
McDougal

McTavish
Mickey
Minnie
Mister
Misty
Molly
Mudgee
Nala
Nayia
Oscar
Paddie
Patch
Peggy
Petra
Phoebe
Poppet
Professor
Pugsley
Pym
Rosie
Rowf
Roxy
Ruska
Sadie
Sam
Sandy
Sasha
Scamp
Scott
Scruffy
Sheba
Skye
Spike
Spot
Susie
Suzie
Tammy
Ted

Tessa
Tipsy
Toffy
Zac
Zoe

TIBETAN SPANIEL
Kimba
Sengay

TIBETAN TERRIER
Alice
Brandy
Llasha
Ludo
Miranda
Tessa

WEIMARANER
Beau
Budd
Cassie
Clyde
Crystal
Dana
Doug
Duke
Ellie
Greta
Gretel
Jackson
King Titus
Liebchen
Lola
Misty
Mudgee
Oliver
Rudi

Sasha
Tessa
Tilly
Willy
Zoe

WEIMERANER CROSS
Coco
Sid
Spud
Wolfgang

WELSH CORGI CARDIGAN
Amy
Brandy
Cindy
Deli
Donna
Honey
Midge
Peter
Rocky
Sooki
Specks
Toby
Trixi
Wooly

WELSH SPRINGER SPANIEL
Annie
Eric
Jake
Jasper
Rudi
Sam

WELSH TERRIER
Merri
Toby

WEST HIGHLAND WHITE
Aberdeen
Angus
Basil
Bonnie
Buttons
Darby
Dougal
Emily
Fergus
Hamish
Jessie
Joli
Kaitlin
Katie
Lachlan
Laddie
Lilly
Macbeth
Mcduff
Muffy
Ralph
Sandy
Scottie
Shionach
Tamus
Teddy

WHIPPET
Athena
Elle
Felix
Freddy

Henry
Minky
Oberon
Smokey
Topaz
Whippet
Whippy
Wink
Winny

WHIPPET CROSS
Coco
Daisy
Homer
Penny
Piglet
Tiffany
Whiskey
Ziggy

WOLFHOUND CROSS
Moet
Sparky
Wolfie

YORKSHIRE TERRIER
Alice
Ben
Bonzi
Bubush
Buffy
Chanel
Danny
Muffin
Pugsley
Ripley
Roger

Sandy
Scrappy
Scruffy
Sean
Tammy
Trevor
Wendy
Wilbur
Wombat

CATS

ABYSSINIAN
Abbey
Abby
Akina
Annabelle
Azja
Caesar
Casablanca
Chelsea
Chloe
Frankie
Gomez
Ilai
Jack
Mia

Oki
Peppi
Pharoah
Sam
Sappho
Scarob
Shashe
Star
Syninan
Tawny Tesse
Tawny Tikee
Tawny Tillee
Tut
Wolf
Zilog

ABYSSINIAN CROSS
Abba
Blossom
Boney
Boofhead
Cat
Cosmo
Erik
Ginger
Abby
Hugo
Josephine
Kitty-Cat
Mickey

Minky
Portia
Shar
Tangles
Texas
Tiger
Toby
Tom Kitten
Whinger

BALINESE
Baggins
Bali
Blossom
Coco
Holly
Kami
Samson
Tasha

BENGAL
Kimba
Rani

BIRMAN
Ashanti
Barnie
Buffy
Cappi
Carmen
Cassie
Charlie Brown
Chloe
Chubbs
Chungfu
Coco
Cognac
Cosmo

Estelle
Fluffy
Harley
Harry
Holly
Jack
Jason
Jasper
Katie
Ki
Kimba
Lucy
Maddie
Marcus
Mia
Milo
Ming
Mischa
Mitsu
Nannuk
Neischa
Neisha
Niska
Oscar
Pastel
Pebbles
Peter Pan
Ping
Pong
Pussy Cooma
Rana
Rosie
Samui
Shakespeare
Shan
Shigh
Sidney
Sinbad

Smooch
Stjohn
Su-Lin
Tamil
Tanamera
Ty
Vince
Wilbur
Xie Xie
Zac

BIRMAN CROSS
Kitten
Tanzy

BOMBAY

Bib
Bub

BRITISH BLUE
Daisy
Monza
Oscar
Pod
Thaidy
Watson
Zachary
Zoe

BRITISH SHORTHAIR
Arfer
Cricket
Felicity
Horace
Jemma
Levi
Lord

115

Mackinnon
Lucy
Minnie
Misty
Mulberry
Sacha
Seymour
Sunny
Tammy
Zoe

BURMESE
A C
Ace
Adjani
Ali Khan
Amah
Amber
Ambrose
Anastasia
Andretti
Andy
Angelique
Angus
Anike
Anouche
Arjuna
Arnie
Ash
Ashok
Asja
Augustus
Azzaza
Bachi
Baci
Bailey
Baja
Bajimby

Bam-Bam
Bambi
Banjo
Barnaby
Barney
Basil
Bazer
Bear
Beau
Becky
Bella
Belle
Ben
Benji
Benny
Benoir
Bess
Big Doodie
Bill
Bimba
Bindi
Binti
Biscuit
Blue Boy
Bobby
Bogart
Boris
Bronson
Bronte
Brown Cat
Bruce
Bubbles
Bud
Buddy
Buffy
Bundy
Buster
Buzz

Byron
C C
Caddie
Caesar
Cagney
Caitlin
Capuccino
Carlos
Casey
Casper
Cat
Caveat
Cecil
Ceena
Chairo
Champas
Champers
Chanel
Charlie
Charlie Brown
Charlie Gray
Cheeky
Chilli
Chip
Chloe
Chocci
Chocky
Choco
Chocolate
Chocolate
  Cake
Choo Choo
Chots
Chow
Christabel
Cindy
Claude
Cleo

Clousseau
Coca Cola
Coco
Cointreau
Collingwood
Concerto
Cookie
Cosby
Crystal
Cybil
Czar
Darcy
Darling
Delice
Dewi
Dillie
Dillon
Dolly Varden
Domus
Donna
Dudley
Ebee
Ellie
Elliot
Elsa
Enya
Eric
Eartha Kitt
Fin
Fluffy
Foss
Frances
Frank
Franki
Freckles
Freddo
Friska
Fritz

Fudge
Garry
Gibbitty
Grace
Grotty
Gus
Hamlet
Hana
Harley
Hazel
Hector
Hendo
Hermes
Hobi
Honey
Horace
Houdini
Indiana
Iris
Isabel
Isobella
Jaala
Jack
Jake
Janis
Jasmine
Jasper
Jeannie
Jedda
Jemma
Jenny
Jerry
Jessica
Jessie
Jet
Jethro
Jimbi
Jimmy

Jing
John
Jonsie
Julius
Kaffa
Kahlua
Kaitlyn
Kal
Kalib
Kao
Katina
Kayja
Keira
Khan
Kim
Kipper
Kippling
Kiri
Kitten
Ko Ki
Koto
Kotyk
Kracker Jack
Kylah
Lady Kathleen
Lana
Laxmi

117

NAME YOUR PET!

Leah	Micky	Noisette
Leo	Midnight	Olli
Leonie	Milo	Oscar
Lilla	Mimi	Ottie
Lilly	Ming	Otto
Ling	Minky	Paddy
Lotus	Minou	Pagan
Louise	Mischa	Parker
Lu Lu	Misha	Patrick
Lucinda	Missy	Pearly
Lucy	Mist	Pendragon
Luka	Misty	Pepe
Lutz	Mitze	Peppa
M P	Moisha	Pepper
Mac	Mollie	Perina
Madali Suki	Molly	Phantom
Maisie	Mona	Phoebe
Mao	Monte	Pippin
Marcus	Monty	Polo
Martha	Mooshi	Ponti
Martisse	Moriyz	Pookie
Marzipan	Moth	Poppy
Matilda	Mouska	Porscha
Matty	Mozart	Princess
Max	Mr Cat	Priscilla
Maxine	Muffin	Pugsly
Maybel	Murphy	Purdie
Meeko	Musetta	Purdita
Meg	Mystique	Purrseus
Megsy	Napoleon	Purrson
Melanzane	Natasha	Pushka
Mephisto	Necki	Puss
Mercedes	Neil	Pussy
Merlin	Nessy	Raj
Merlina	Nicki	Rama
Mia	Nicky	Rameses
Micah	Nicole	Ranee
Michi	Nimue	Rangi

Rangoon	Sheba	Tara
Rani	Shelly	Tasha
Rebel	Shimbi	Te-Amo
Rhama	Shiva	Ted
Ricki	Sian	Teddy Bear
Rocket	Sid	Tela
Roger	Silver	Tessa
Roly	Simba	Thani
Rosetta	Sinbad	Thea
Rosie	Sirach	Thelma
Rowdy	Skinny	Tia
Ruhfus	Snookie	Tierney
Sabella	Sonia	Tigga
Sacha	Soo	Tigger
Saki	Sooty	Tikka
Sally	Sophie	Tilin
Sam	Spatz	Tim
Samantha	Splash	Tina
Samba	Spooky	Titch
Samisen	Spud	Toby
Sampson	Squizzie	Tomkinson
Samson	Squizzy	Tootsie
Sandi	Steve	Top Cat
Sangupor	Su Su	Tory
Sapphire	Suki	Tosca
Sarah	Sultan	Trashy
Sardi	Sumba	Trinket
Sascha	Sushi	Tsien
Sasha	Suvi	Tugger
Schamus	Suzie	Tuna
Schon	Sybil	Twiggy
Sebastian	Sydney	Twinky
Seeto	Tai	Victoria
Serano	Tamina	Wanda
Shakira	Tamsen	Whisper
Shamar	Tango	Willy
Shannon	Tansy	Zac
Shattwo	Tao	Zak

Zamandalay
Zarlee
Zeba
Ziggy
Zoe
Zoltan
Zsa Zsa

CHINCHILLA

Archie
Arnie
Arpege
Baggy
Bella
Benji
Bimba
Casper
Cassiopoea
Chilla
Chilli
Chin Chin
Coco
Crystal
Darling
Felix
Jade

Jessie
Juliette
Maxine
Millie
Misty
Moe
Moet
Monty
Muppy
Nathan
Nikita
Oscar
Pixie
Pookie
Princess
Priscilla
Pudding
Puss
Rabbit
Regae
Rosie
Sallyann
Samantha
Sammy
Samson
Sausage
Sebastian
Shiroi
Simba
Snowy
Solomon
Sophie
Taboo
Tahnee
Tishea
Toby
Tommy
Winston

Yoda
Zoe

CORNISH REX

Canleigh
E T
Mojo
Mr T
Smudge

CORNISH REX CROSS

Mojo
Rex
Spooky

CROSS BURMESE

Aerial
Aicha
Allie
Baxter
Bright Eyes
Buttercup
Cfor
Chloe
Ebony
Elliot
Els
Elsie
Friday
Fritz
Gomez
Gumnut
Gus
Honey
J D
Josiah
Kitty

Lila
Lucky
Meggs
Mischa
Misty
Moet
Monnie
Mozart
Mr Chloe
Mudcrab
Myrrh
Patsy
Samson
Sasha
Sebastian
Shmee
Smokey
Sylvester
Tassie
Tazi
T C
Tex
Victoria
Whiskers

DEVON REX
Beauchamp
Chloe
Devon Rex
Doris
Gizmo
Jake
Leroy
Lulu
Mindy
Mintie
Morgan
Moses

Mulder
Noddy
Phoebe
Raffles
Scully
Skye
Ziggy

DEVON REX
CROSS
Max

DOMESTIC LONG
HAIR
Abbie
Abigail
Alberquerque
Alec
Alike
Alley
Amber
Angela
Annie
April
Audrey
Aurora
Aussie
Bandit
Banjo
Bega
Benjamin
Benji
Benny
Bertie
Bijoux
Bimbo
Black
Black Cat

Black Kitten
Blackie
Blackout
Bonnie
Boris
Bow
Bronte
Bub
Bullwinkle
Cally
Casper
Cat
Charlotte
Chas
Che Che Bella
Chintz
Chloe
Cindy
Cleo
Cleopatra
Cookie
Crystal
Daisy
Darcey
Deana
Dinky
Ducatti
Dudley
Duffy
Eden
Eric
Ertha
Fergie
Flossy
Fluff
Fluffy
Foxy
Frankie

NAME YOUR PET!

Fred	Leila	Nala
Fudge	Lily	Napoleon
Garfield	Louie	Natasha
George	Lucy	Neungy
Ginger Megs	Luke	Norman
Gingy	Lulu	Nutmeg
Gizzy	Mad	Odie
Gucci	Magnus	Odin
Hamish	Maisy	Ollie
Hannah	Marion	Oops
Harley	Marzipan	Orlando
Harry	Mave	Oscar
Honey	Max	Paddy Fin
Hugo	Meggs	Paladin
Indy	Meggsie	Paul
Inky	Megsy	Peachy
J D	Mickey	Pebbles
Jamie	Midy	Penny
Jardy	Millie	Pepe
Jasmine	Minka	Phantom
Jazz	Minnie	Phoebe
Jerry	Minou	Pickles
Jessica	Mischa	Piddles
Jessie	Mischka	Plunkett
Jo Jo	Mishka	Pokie
Joanne	Missy	Polly
Jose	Misty	Povorino
Josie	Mitzi	Puffin
Julius	Mogsy	Purrdy
Kalua	Molly	Pushka
Katie	Mona	Puss
Kimmy	Monty	Pussy
Kitty	Moses	Pussy Willow
Klaus	Mother	Ralph
Koshka	Muffin	Raoul
Kotka	Muffy	Rascal
Laura	Mufti	Rebel
Leah	Murphy	Rex

Rimini
Rocky
Rosebud
Ruby
Rudi
Sacha
Sadie
Sally
Sam
Sandy
Sarah
Sasha
Scabby
Schnule
Scotty
Scrap
Scully
Scwuffy
Shadow
Shelley
Shminki
Silvester
Simba
Small Fry
Smokey
Snooky
Snuffles
Sooty
Sophie

Spinach
Spud
Squiggy
Stinky
Sunshine
Sylvia
Tangerine
Tarquin
Thomas
Tiger
Tigger
Tinkerbell
Tip
Tippy
Toddles
Truffles
Turbo
Twig
Victor
Violet
Wicky Woo
Willow
Willy
Winnie
Wolf
Woosie
Yang
Zelda
Zoe
Zu Zu

**DOMESTIC
SHORTHAIR**
A J
Abbey
Abbie
Abbott
Abby

Abigail
Ada
Adelaide
Adeva
Aero
Al
Albert
Alberta
Alec
Alex
Alexander
Alfie
Alfred
Ali
Alice
Allethea
Alley
Amber
Amelia
Amon-Ra
Amy
Anastasia
Andy
Angel
Angelica
Angie
Angus
Anki
Annabelle
Annie
Aphro
April
Arabella
Archie
Argenta
Argyle
Arjuna
Armaggedon

Arnie
Arnold
Art
Ash
Asher
Ashleigh
Aspen
Atticus
Aussie
B T
Babagnoosh
Babe
Babette
Babs
Baby
Babygirl
Bacchus
Baci
Baggy
Bagheera
Bailey
Baileys
Baldrick
Ballou
Bambi
Barney
Barnie
Barry
Bart
Basil
Basilcat
Batcat
Batman
Bazil
Bazza
Bea
Beam
Beans

Bear
Beatrice
Beau
Beau Beau
Beau K
Becky
Bee
Bee Gee
Bella
Belle
Bells
Ben
Benjamin
Benji
Benny
Benson
Bentley
Berber
Bernie
Berry
Bert
Bertolli
Bessie
Betsy
Betty
Bianca
Bianco
Bibby
Bibs
Biddy
Biff
Biffy
Big Black Cat
Big Puss
Biggles
Biily
Bilbo
Bill

Billie
Billy
Bindi
Bindy
Bing
Bingo
Binky
Biskit
Black & White
Black Baby
Black Cat
Black Jack
Black White
Blackett
Blackie
Blacky
Blinkey
Blitzen
Blossom
Blossum
Blue
Bluey
Bo
Bo Bo
Bob
Bobbie
Bobby
Bobby Sox
Bobcat
Bodie
Bogey
Boj
Bondy
Boney
Bonnie
Bonny
Boof
Boofhead

Bootie
Booker
Booky
Boots
Bootsie
Booty
Boral
Boris
Boston
Boy
Boynton
Boz
Bracken
Brandy
Brian
Bright Eyes
Brin
Brioche
Brookie
Brownie
Bruce
Brummel
Bruno
Bruser
Brutus
Bubble
Bubbles
Bubi
Bud
Buffy
Buggles
Buik
Bulla
Bully
Bumper
Bundle
Bunny
Burnie

Burt
Bus
Busby
Buster
Busy
Butch
Butterball
Buttercup
Buttons
Buzz
Bwana
C
C C
C for
Cactus
Caesar
Calico
Cally
Calypso
Candy
Cara
Caramel
Carlos Felipe
Carlton
Carma
Caroline
Carrington
Casey
Casio
Casper
Cass
Cassie
Cassius
Cassper
Cat
Cat-Balloo
Catastrophe
Cecilia

Cephy
Chablis
Chadders
Champus
Chan
Channel
Charles
Charley
Charlie
Charlie Brown
Charlotte
Chatte
Chatters
Checkers
Cheeky
Cheetah
Chelsea
Cherie
Cherrie
Cherub
Chester
Chewbacca
Chewy
Chi Chi
Chilli
Chin Chin
China
Chintz
Chips
Chiquilin
Chloe
Chocolate
Chomsky
Chopin
Chrissy
Christine
Christy
Chucky

NAME YOUR PET!

Church
Cicada
Cimba
Cinamon
Cinderella
Cinders
Cindy
Cinna
Cinnamon
Cisco
Ciska
Claude
Claudius
Claw
Clawed
Clayton
Cleo
Clicquot
Clive
Clix
Clyde
Clydell
Cobber
Coco
Coconut
Cody
Cola

Collingwood
Combat
Consuela
Cookie
Cool
Copper
Corby
Corey
Corky
Corrie
Cosima
Cosmo
Couch
Cougall
Crackers
Crazy
Cristobel
Critter
Croissant
Crumble
Crusty
Crystal
Cuddle Pie
Cuddles
Cuff
Curtis
Curtly
Cush
Custard
Cutie
D J
Daffy
Daisy
Dakota
Daks
Danny
Darlene
Dartagnan

Dave
Deanna
Desi
Devil
Di Di
Diablo
Diasy
Digger
Dingo
Diousse
Dippy
Dolly
Domingo
Donut
Doodie
Dopey
Dorcas
Doris
Dorothy
Dot
Dotty
Douglas
Drummer
Dudley
Dusky
Dusty
Dylan
E T
Ebby
Ebony
Eddie
Eddy
Edward
Eedra
Electra
Eleesha
Eli
Elijah

Elizabeth	Flora	Georgina
Elle	Flossie	Gerald
Elliot	Floyd	Geri
Elly	Fluffy	Gerry
Elmo	Fonzie	Gertie
Elmo Arnold	Foofoo	Gertrude
Elsa	Fossey	Gfor
Elvis	Foster	Gi Gi
Emerald	Foufette	Gibs
Emily	Fove	Gidget
Emma	Fox	Gina
Emma Bronte	Foxie	Ging
Emmy	Fozdik	Ginge
Eponine	Fozzie	Ginger
Eric	Frank	Ginger Cat
Erik	Frankie	Ginger Meggs
Ernest	Franky	Ginger Mickey
Errol	Frascati	Ginger Paws
Essy	Frazer	Gingus
Etc	Freckles	Ginney
Fang	Fred	Ginny
Farrah	Freda	Gismo
Fat Cat	Freddy	Gizmo
Fatso	Freya	Gizzmo
Felicity	Friday	Gizzy
Felix	Frisky	Gnocci
Feliz	Fritz	Gobelino
Femmie	Fu	Goldie
Fergus	Fudge	Goldilocks
Festy	Fuschia	Golly
Fidel	Galaderiel	Googy Egg
Fifi	Garfield	Gordon
Figaro	Garp	Gordon
Finn	Gary	Bennett
Finnigan	Gatto Pardo	Gracie
Fitzy	Gemma	Graham
Flee	George	Granite
Fletch	Georgie	Gregory

NAME YOUR PET!

Gremlin	Honey	Belmonde
Grey	Horace	Jeannie
Greymalken	Horatio	Jellicoe
Grimaldi	Howard	Jemima
Gucci	Huang	Jemimah
Guinness	Humphey	Jemma
Gummi	Humphrey	Jenny
Gus	Hungry	Jeremiah
Gypsy	Ichabod	Jerome
H G	Inca	Jerry
Haju	Indi	Jess
Halley	India	Jesse
Hamish	Indiana	Jessica
Hank	Indra	Jessie
Hara	Inky	Jester
Harlem	Isaac	Jet
Harley	Isabella	Jet Cat
Harold	Isabelle	Jezabel
Harrier	Itchy	Jilly
Harriet	Itchy Boy	Jim
Harriette	Izzy	Jiminy
Harrison	Jack	Jindy
Harry	Jackson	Jo Jo
Harvey	Jacquii	Jock
Hastings	Jaffa	Jodie
Heidi	Jaguar	Joe
Henritta	Jake	Joey
Henry	Jamal	John Candy
Herbert	Jamali	Johnnie
Hercules	Janey	Johnny
Hero	Janx	Johnson
Hexagon	Jasmine	Jojo
Hilary	Jason	Josh
Hilda	Jasper	Joshua
Hildergard	Jaxon	Josie
Hitam	Jay	Juanita
Hobbs	Jazz	Judy
Holly	Jean Clawed	Julia

Julius
K 2
Ka
Kahlua
Kami
Kanga
Kashmir
Kasi
Kate
Katerina
Katie
Kato
Katsu
Katy
Kay
Kay Dee
Kazamir
Keiffer
Keisha
Kelly
Ken
Ketty
Khan
Khani
Killer
Kim
Kimba
Kimmy
Kinda
Kingston
Kiri
Kirsten
Kissa
Kit
Kitt
Kitten
Kitty
Kitty Cat

Kitty Kat
Kitty Litter
Kiwi
Knickers
Knuckle
Koshka
Kotka
Kratzerli
Kristy
Krystol
Kucing
Kunta
Kusack
Kuss Kuss
Kymber
L A
Lady
Lamington
Langford
Lara
Larry
Laser
Laura
Laurel
Le Roy
Lea
Leanna
Lear
Ledge
Lelik
Lenny
Leo
Leopard
Lettie
Levi-Rose
Lewa
Lewis
Lexi

Lexy
Lia
Libby
Lickety
Licorice
Liesl
Lightning
Lil Pudd
Lilly
Linus
Lisa
Little Cat
Little Diddle -
   King
Little Guy
Little Kitty
Little Puddy
Little Puss
Little Tabby
Littley
Lizzie
Lodger
Logan
Loki
Lola
Lolita
Lolly
Lonely
Long Tail
Lotte
Louis
Lovey
Lowanna
Lowry
Loxy
Lucas
Lucille
Lucinda

NAME YOUR PET!

Lucky	Maow	Megs
Lucky Tom	Mapp	Meia
Lucy	Marco	Meisje
Luka	Margwa	Melanie
Luke	Marlow	Melba
Luli	Marmaduke	Melbourne
Lulu	Marmalade	Meow
Mabilu	Marnix	Mercedes
Mac	Marta	Mergatroyd
Macduff	Martha	Merinda
Macina	Marty	Merlin
Macro	Marvey	Merp
Madam	Mary	Mia
Maddison	Marylyn	Michael
Maddy	Marzipan	Michelle
Madge	Mascara	Mickey
Madison	Maschka	Micki
Madonna	Mason	Micky
Maggie	Matilda	Middy
Maggie May	Matt	Midnight
Magnum	Mau Mau	Miffy
Mahjong	Maude	Mike
Maisy	Maudie	Mikey
Mallet	Maurice	Mikki
Malmi	Maverick	Mildew
Mambo	Max	Miles
Mami	Maxine	Millie
Manchy	Maxwell	Milly
Mandarin	May-Lee	Milo
Mandarley	Mayake	Mimi
Mandu	Mayo	Mince
Mandy	M C	Minchinbury
Mango	Mctavish	Mindi
Manly	Meg	Mindy
Mannix	Meggie	Ming
Manuel	Meggs	Ming Ming
Mao	Meggsie	Mingus
Mao Mao	Meggy	Mini

Mink
Minka
Minke
Minkey
Minkie
Minky
Minney
Minnie
Minnie Mouse
Minou
Minsky
Minstral
Minxie
Mischa
Mischief
Mischka
Mish
Misha
Mishca
Mishkar
Mishy
Miss Prissy
Missie
Mission
Missy
Mista
Misty
Misty Puss
Mitsy
Mitty
Mitzi
Mitzy
Mo
Moet
Moey
Mog
Mogg
Moggie

Moggy
Mollie
Molly
Mon
Monday
Monet
Mongee
Monie
Monkey
Monster
Montana
Monte
Monty
Moo
Mooch
Mook
Moose
Mooshi
Mooty
Moppet
Morag
Morbell
Morgan
Morris
Morticia
Mortisha
Mosby
Mosey
Moss
Mother
Mother Cat
Motley
Mouse
Mousey
Mousse
Mowgli
Mozart
Mozzi

Mozzie
Mr Border
Mr Cheecky
Mr Conan
Mr Grace
Mr Herriot
Mr Mcphee
Mr Puddy
Mr Smif
Mr Stevens
Mr Stripy
  Pants
Mr T
Mr Tom Wong
Mrs Bones
Mrs Cleo Puss
Mrs Puss
Muff
Muffin
Muffins
Muffy
Munchie
Munchkin
Mungo
Murgatroyd
Murph
Murphy
Musetta
Mushie

Mushka	Numpsi	Patchy
Mushroom	Nutmeg	Patrick
Mushy	Nutty	Pattie
Musket	Oberon	Pavarotti
Mutley	Ocho	Peaches
Mutt	Octo	Pear
Mystique	Odie	Pearl
Mystra	Olive	Pebbles
Nala	Oliver	Pedra
Nancy	Olivia	Pedro
Natasha	Ollie	Peggy
Nathaniel	Olly	Pele
Natsu	Oopsy	Pelham
Naughty	Ophelia	Penny
Navi	Ophie	Pepe
Nefertiti	Opie	Pepi
Neffa	Orange	Pepper
Neko	Orlando	Peppy
Nelson	Oscar	Pepy
Nermal	Oska	Percy
Nero	Othello	Perry
Nessie	Otto	Pesh
Netty	Owl	Pesto
Nicki	P	Pesty
Nicky	P C	Pete
Nike	Pablo	Peter
Nim	Paddles	Peter Polly
Nina	Paddo	Petunia
Ning	Paddy	Phantom
Ninja	Paint Tin	Philamena
Nishi	Paloma	Phoebe
Noni	Panda	Phoenix
Noody	Pantha	Phremy
Nori	Panther	Piatza
Norm	Paris	Picasso
Norman	Parker	Pickles
Nouscha	Patch	Pie
Nudge	Patches	Piffany

Pillin	Puce	Queenie
Pimms	Pucin	Quincy
Ping Pong	Pud	Quiver
Pinocchio	Pudding	Radar
Pippa	Puddles	Railene
Pippi	Puddup	Rain
Pippin	Puddy	Rainbow
Pippy	Puddy Cat	Rajah
Pitch	Puddy Puddy	Ralph
Pixel	Pudgie	Rambo
Pixie	Puffin	Ranee
Playful	Pug	Rani
Pluto	Pugsley	Raphael
Podgy	Pumpkin	Rascal
Pokey	Punter	Rasmus
Polly	Pure White	Rat
Pone	Pushka	Ratu
Pongo	Pushkin	Raynor
Poo	Pushush	Raz
Pooch	Pushy	Rebecca
Pooh	Puska	Rebel
Pooky	Puss	Reebok
Poppy	Puss In Boots	Reggie
Popsy	Puss Puss	Remus
Portia	Puss-Puss	Rex
Poss	Pussca	Richard
Possum	Pusscat	Richie
Pounce	Pussi	Rick
Prancer	Pussum	Rin Tin
Pratchett	Pussy	Rip Rak
Pretzel	Pussy Cat	Ripley
Prince	Pussy Poppett	Ripples
Princess	Pussycat	River
Priscilla	Pussyfoot	Robin
Prowler	Pusvwa	Robyn
Prudence	Puto	Rocklilly
Prufrock	Puzzle	Rocky
Psyche	Quality	Rodney

NAME YOUR PET!

Roger
Roland
Romeo
Rommel
Romulus
Ronnie
Roo
Rory
Rose
Rosey
Rosi
Rosie
Rowland
Roxanne
Ru
Ruby
Rudy
Ruffles
Rufus
Rugger
Rumples
Rumpole
Rumpus
Rupert
Rupes
Ruprect
Ruski
Russkie
Rusty
S B
Sable
Sabrina
Sade
Sadie
Sage
Sally
Salt & Pepper
Sam

Samantha
Sammy
Sampson
Samson
Samuel
Sandy
Sansha
Santa
Sapphie
Sara
Sarah
Sash
Sasha
Sassy
Satchmo
Saul
Sauren
Saxon
Scamp
Scardy
Scarlet
Schubert
Scooter
Scrap
Scratch
Scratchy
Scruff
Scruffy
Scrumpy
Sean
Seaview
Sebastian
Selena
Selina
Shadow
Shakti
Shammy
Shamus

Shan
Shani
Sheba
Sheila
Shelford
Shelley
Shelly
Sherman
Shiralee
Shirley
Shortie
Shula
Shushi
Siam
Sid
Sidney
Silky
Silvy
Simba
Simby
Simon
Skeeta
Skelm
Sketty
Skippy
Skisto

Skitso	Sooty	Stokes
Skittles	Sophie	Stomper
Skitty Cat	Souffle	Storm
Skitzo	Sox	Strawberry
Sky	Soxie	Stray Mum
Slinky	Soxy	Streaker
Slivia	Space Cat	Strumpet
Smakka	Sparkles	Stumpy
Smokey	Sparky	Stupe
Smokey Bear	Spats	Stupid
Smooch	Spaz	Sugar
Smoose	Speedo	Suki
Smudge	Speedwell	Sula
Snippets	Spider	Sultan
Snitty	Spike	Sunny
Snooky	Spikey	Sunshine
Snoops	Spinner	Susie
Snoopy	Spirit	Suzi
Snootzie	Spit	Suzuka
Snorkel	Splotch	Suzy
Snow Beau	Spock	Sweet Emma
Snowball	Spook	Sweet Pea
Snowflake	Spooky	Sweetie Puss
Snowhite	Spot	Swift
Snowy	Spotty	Sybella
Snuffles	Sprocket	Syd
Snuffy	Spud	Sydney
Snugglepot	Spunky	Sylvesta
Snuggler	Sqeaky	Sylvester
Snuggles	Squeak	Sylvia
Socks	Squeaker	Sylvie
Soda	Squeaky	Sylvy
Sonny	Squib	Szupi
Sook	Squidgy	T C
Sooki	Stanley	Tabatha
Sooky	Stella	Tabby
Sootica	Stetson	Tabby Man
Sootie	Stimpy	Tabby White

135

NAME YOUR PET!

Tablet
Tabs
Tabsy
Tacha
Tacking
Taffy
Taj
Tamara
Tammy
Tandy
Tangles
Tango
Tania
Tanj-It
Tanka
Tara
Tash
Tasha
Tassie
Tates
Tattles
Taz
Teaka
Teddy
Teeny
Tercia
Terry
Tesha
Tess
Tessa
Tessie
The Butler
Thirteen
Thomas
Thomasina
Thumper
Thunder
Tibby

Ticky
Tico
Tiddler
Tiddles
Tiffany
Tiga
Tiger
Tiger Puss
Tigga
Tigger
Tigger Puss
Tiggs
Tiggy
Tigsey
Tiki
Tillie
Tilly
Tim
Timmy
Tin Tin
Tina
Tinka
Tinker
Tinkerbell
Tinky
Tinsel
Tiny
Tippets
Tippi
Tippy
Tipsy
Tish
Tisha
Tishka
Titch Too
Tituba
Titus
Tobias

Toby
Toddy
Toffee
Tokolosh
Tom
Tom Tom
Tomcat
Tomkit
Tommy
Tonto
Tooley
Tootie
Toots
Tootsie
Topaz
Topsy
Tora
Tortie
Tortise
Tortoi
Torty
Tosca
Tosh
Toshi
Touche
Toxo
Toya
Trebor
Trelawney
Trevour
Trigger
Trini
Tristan
Trixie
Tujo
Tunguska
Tuppence
Tuppenny

Tuppy
Tuscot
Tutan
Tux
Tuxy
Tweedle Dum
Tweety
Twiddle
Twiddle Dee
Twiggy
Twinkle
Twinkles
Tyla
Vahine
Valentine
Valentino
Vegemite
Venus
Vesta
Victor
Vince
Vincent
Vinnie
Violet
Viv
Voila
Waif
Walgett
Wally
Wanda
Wayne
Weadle
Wesley
Wheely
Whiffy
Whingy
Whiskas
Whiskers

Whiskey
Whisky
Whisper
White Cat
Whitey
Whitney
Whoopi
Whoopie
Wilbur
Wilbur-Puss
William
Willie
Willow
Willy
Wilma
Wincy
Winkie
Winkle
Winnie
Winnipeg
Winston
Wolf
Wombat
Woody
Woosel
Woosie
Wooso
Worry
Xanthor
Yana
Yang
Yeti
Yo Yo
Yorik
Zac
Zach
Zachary
Zack

Zag
Zane
Zap
Zapp
Zazu
Zebedee
Zebie
Zena
Zenzi
Zig
Ziggy
Zinzan
Zip
Zipper
Zippy
Zodia
Zoe
Zonk
Zorro
Zulee
Zulu
Zumi

FOREIGN WHITE
Boris
Cassy
Hovie
Surfy

HIMALAYAN
Alex
Alley
Ama
Ayla
Azuree
Baby
Bachi
Baci

NAME YOUR PET!

Bangles
Barnabus
Beau
Ben
Billy Boy
Billie
Bluebell
Bobbie
Bonnie
Boofy
Buster
Calico
Cameo
Casper
Chalu
Chanette
Charlie
Chloe
Christie
Clarence
Claude
Clinton
Coco
Cosworth
Czar
Daisy
Ebony
Emby
Fire & Ice

Flossie
Fluffy
Gismo
Gizmo
Gulliver
Gumby
Gypsy
Harley
Heidi
Hobie
Jade
Jasmine
Kahlua
Karma
Katmandu
Khasha
Kishma
Kitten
Kyra
Little Mittens
Little One
Lladro
Lu Lu
Maddison
Mandu
Max
Merlie
Milo
Ming
Minkie
Minky
Minty
Missy
Misty
Moonbeam
Morse
Morse Code
Muffin

Muffy
Mum Puss
Musket
Nicky
Nushka
Nutmeg
Ollie
Oscar
Ozzy
Pebbles
Persephone
Petite Toutou
Phantom
Pip
Polar
Porridge
Primrose
Ralph
Rama
Randi
Saki
Sam
Samantha
Sammy
Sarah
Sassy
Sheba
Sheema
Shimi
Silvester
Smokey
Snow
Sparky
Squadgy
Tabby
Taki
Tamiko
Thumper

138

Tiddly Pom
Tinkerbell
Tiny
Toga
Tosca
Whelan
Wolfgang
Yeti
Yoshi

HIMALAYAN
CROSS
B B
Bibby
Calvin
Cindy
Coco
Geordie
Max
Millie
Mister
Nuts
Pixie
Poncie
Purcy
Rascal
Rose Petals
Simon
Sophie

KORAT
Dakota
Lulu
Timmy

MAINE COON
Soda
Toffilees

Whiskey

MANX
Houdini
Jasmine

ORIENTAL
SHORTHAIR
Beau
Boris
Felix
Freycinet
Jingles
Kiri
Ling Ling
Napoleon
Penelope
Portia
Sammy
Shazam
Sootie
Sultan
Vincent
Wesley
Zorro

PERSIAN
Alex
Amanda
Anastasia
Annie
Anooshka
Anuschka
Apollo
Arnold
Arthur
Autumn
Baba

Barnaby
Becky
Bella
Belle
Benjamin
Benji
Black
Boston
Bubbles
C C
Calvin
Casper
Cassie
Chi Chi
Chloe
Cladagh
Crystal
Cuddles
Debonair
Diamond
Dweezel
Emily
Fatso
Felix
Franklin
Fred
Gi Gi
Gismo
Gizmo
Harley
Harry
Honey
Isabel
Isabella
Ivo
Jacques
Kimba
Kiri

NAME YOUR PET!

Kitten
Krista
Layla
Louis
Luce
Maisy
Max
Mickey
Mischka
Misha
Misty
Mitzi
Moet
Monty
Mozart
Muffin
Muffy
Mugwai
Nini
Orange Boy
Oscar
Oz
Ozzie
Paladin
Pepe
Peri
Persia
Phoebe
Princess
Priscilla
Puff
Pumpkin
Pushkin
Rahjie
Romeo
Saber
Sabrina
Sam

Samantha
Sammy
Sibalius
Siggi
Sky
Snowflake
Sooty
Sunny
Suzie
Suzy
Tahsha
Tara
Taylor
Tiga
Topsy
Willy
Winston
Zeus
Zi Zi

PERSIAN CROSS
Alex
Amber
Annabel
Bees Wax
Bob
Bondi
Bruiser
Buster
Caesar
Candy
Cassius
Champers
Charlie
Cindy
Cleo
Coco
Dillon

Dusty
Floosie
Fluffy
Frangipani
Fritz
Greta
Jango
Jazz
Jesse
Jock
Jolly
Kimba
Kitty
Kitty-Angel
Kuching
Kus Kus
Lola
Lulu
Marmite
Max
Megs
Millie
Mimi
Mindi
Mishi
Missy
Misty
Moet
Monster
Mottley
Murphy
Natasha
Nero
P.C
Pedro
Persia
Popcorn
Poppet

140

Pushkin
Pye
Ratty
Raven
Roly
Sam
Samantha
Sarah
Scampy
Shmitten
Silky
Silly
Sobella
Sparky
Squid
Susie
Tasha
Ted
Thomas
Tigger
Tiki
Timothy
Top Cat
Winston

RAGDOLL
Jason

RUSSIAN BLUE
Annie
Antonina
Bagel
Boris
Brat Cat
Coco
Dela
Duk
Edwina

Kitten
Lucy
Luda
Misty
Molly
Natasha
Nicheka
Nikita
Pavlovich
Puff
Pumpkin
Puss
Ramius
Richenda
Rushkin
Ruska
Sasha
Shenka
Siska
Skye
Tasha
Thomas
Tolstoy
Tzar
Vodka
Woody
Yashka
Yodi

RUSSIAN BLUE CROSS
Boswell
Brat
Dippy
F 19
Jamali
Missy
Misty

Tini

SCOTTISH FOLD
Leeroy
Lord Angus

SIAMESE
Alinta
Andy
Anna
Annabella
Annabelle
Annie
Attila
Baby
Bach
Baci
Ban Ban
Ben
Bianca
Billy
Blue Bell
Bluey
C.C
Cairo
Cara
Carita
Carmen
Casey
Cassidy
Cat
Celine
Chad
Charlie
Charlotte
Chi
Chilli
Chloe

NAME YOUR PET!

Cisca
Cleo
Coco
Cooee
Cori
D J
David
Dennis
Diana
Dolly
Dorothy
Einstein
Elle
Emma Peel
Eso
Everest
Frusty
Gilbert
Gina
Gindy
Giovanni
Gizmo
Gogo
Haggis
Hamlet
Harry
Hattie

Heidi
Hound
Jack
Jai
Jaques
Jasmine
Jazz
Jerlisa
Jezebel
Jossie
Juan
Kali
Kalua
Ketut
Kimba
Kins
Koko
Kushka
Ling
Lisa
Little Doodie
Little Girl
Lloyd
Lonesome
Lou
Lucy
Lui
Mai Tai
Mandy
Marcus
Marley
Matilda
Maxy
Maynard
Mischa
Misty
Moet
Monty

Mung
Musette
Necka
Nichi
Nijinski
Nippity
Noki
Obi
Ollie
Orlando
Oska
Pablo
Pasha
Penny
Pipi
Pittzi
Poppy
Possum
Prince
Princess
Puck
Puhd
Puss
Puss Puss
Pussy
Ra
Rafeke
Rajah
Rambo
Rodger
Roger
Rosie
Rosko
Rubens
Sachi
Sam
San
Sandy

142

Sapphire
Sara
Sasha
Sayam
Scilla
Scratch
Sebastian
Shackera
Shaman
Shapachou
Sheba
Si
Simon
Simone
Skye
Smidgen
Smokey
Solomon
Storm
Suki
Sumo
Taipan
Tami
Tang
Tani
Taniko
Tao
Tara
Targa
Thaie
Thomas
Tia
Tiger
Tinker
Tisha
Toby
Toot
Toy

Violet
Woos
Yasmine
Yum Yum
Zamin
Zazu
Zelda
Zoe

Siamese Cross

Anzac
Bluey
Chloe
Cobweb
Cy
Elle
Gysmo
Jemima
Kissa
Mein
Min
Misty
Monty
Penny
Pitch
Pussy Willow
Sally
Sam
Sarcoma
Shoki
Smokey
Sunshine
Tiger
Veronica
Windy

Somali

Chevy

Desi
Katja
Lion
Oscar
Smokey
Spike
Suki

Spotted Mist

April
Bronte
Jessica
Leo
Maki
Misty
Oscar
Peewee
Phoenix
Rex
Sam
Sasha
Tilly
Tira
Toby

Tonkinese

Basil
Baxter
Benny
Benson
Bilbo
Blanche
Bonny
Buster
Campo
Chat
Cherry
Chisel

143

NAME YOUR PET!

Cinnamon
Cita
Claude
Coco
Coconut
Dooey
Dusty
Gemma
Goose
Jack
Jemma
Julius
Kahlua
Max

Maxine
Minka
Mischa
Moet
Mona
Muffin
Oscar
Rama
Rocky
Rosencrantz
Sabre
Sebastian
Sharne
Sirkit

Smudge
Soe
Sylvester
T C
Tara
Tonk
Tonka
Vincent
Willie
Zoe

TURKISH VAN
Auriel
Peaches

NAMES BY THEMES

AUSTRALIANA

Adelaide
Anzac
Aussie
B1
B2
Banjo
Barrumundi
Barry
Biddy
Bindi
Bindy
Binger
Blinkie
Blossum
Blue
Bluey
Bondi
Bondy
Bonza
Boof
Boofhead
Boofie
Bruce
Brumby
Bubi
Bulla
Charlene
Cicada

Ciggi
Clancy
Cobar
Cobber
Coogee
Crocka
Dax
Digger
Ding
Dingo
Eureka
Fanta
Footy
Freddo
Goanna
Googy Egg
Gum Nuts
Gus
Ivo
Jacko
Jaffa
Kanga
Lamington
Larrikin
Matilda
Mozzie
Mudcrab
Mudgee

Ocker
Oz
Ozzi
Ozzy
Paddo
Possum
Railene
Shiralee
Skippy
Skisto
Snags
Speedo
Steggles
Streuth
Surfy
Swag
Tasman
Tim Tam
Walgett
Weris
Whelan
Whinger
Wombat
Wombi
Womble
Woosie
Wooso
Yamba

RELIGIOUS ORIGIN

Armaggedon
Damien
Deacon

Devil
Diablo
Goliath

Jeremiah
Jezebel
Joshua

Loki
Luther
Nathaniel
Odin
Pagan
Paladin

Rhama
Sampson
Saul
Shaman
Shiva
Siva

Solomon
Spirit
Thor
Voodoo
Zebediah
Zeus

CHARACTER NAMES

Babe
Bagheera
Baldrick
Ballou
Bam-Bam
Bambi
Barney
Batman
Bea
Bo Bo
Bogart
Bogey
Brando
Bronson
Brummel
Bugsy
Bullwinkle
Buster
Cagney
Callan
Carmen
Cassper
Cat-Balloo
Cato
Ceasar
Charlie Brown
Chato
Chewbacca

Chi Chi
Choo Choo
Chuffie
Cinderella
Cinders
Cisco
Conan
Daffy
Darth
Dennis
Dhugal
Dino
Dopey
Dougal
Dr Spock
Elmer
Elwood
Emma Peel
Fivel
Fletch
Flintstone
Fonz
Fonzarelli
Fozzie
Galaderial
Garfield
Gidget
Gigi

Godzilla
Gomez
Gremlin
Gretel
Greymalken
Groover
Grumpy
Gulliver
Hagar
Hamlet
Heathcliff
Heckle
Hector
Heidi
Herbie
Hildergard
Ichabod
Jeckle
Jed
Jemma
Jethro
Kato
Kunta
Lear
Linus
Lochinvar
Lucy Brown
Macbeth

147

Macduff
Magnum
Maverick
Maxwell Smart
Maynard
Mergatroyd
Merlin
Micky
Mindy
Minnie Mouse
Miss Prissy
Mork
Morticia
Mowgli
Mr Happy
Mr McGoo
Mugwai
Mulder
Murgatroyd
Mutley
Nessie
Oberon

Obi
Orlando
Othello
Peabody
Pebbles
Peter Pan
Pinocchio
Poo Bear
Pooh Bear
Popeye
Portia
Prufrock
Pugsley
Rambo
Remington
Rin Tin
Romeo
Rowdy
Rumpole
Ruprect
Sabrina
Schultz

Scoobie
Sengay
Shazam
Sherlock
Simba
Sinbad
Smokey Bear
Snoopy
Snow White
Snowhite
Stimpy
Sylvester
Tonto
Top Cat
Tristan
Tuppy
Woody
Xanthor
Yorik
Zebedee
Zelda
Zorro

COLOUR RELATED

Amber
Azuree
Big Black Cat
Black Baby
Black Cat
Black Jack
Black Night
Blackie
Blondy
Blue Boy
Blue Nell
Brindle

Brown Cat
Brownie
Caramel
Cinamon
Fudge
Ginger
Ginger Abby
Ginger Cat
Ginger Meggs
Ginger Mickey
Ginger Paws
Gingy

Grey Bunny
Grey Ears
Grey Girl
Hazel
Indigo
Orange
Orange Boy
Sky Blue
White Cat
Babygirl
Bear
Bertie

CUTIE

Best Pal
Bilbo
Binkey
Blinkey
Blue Bell
Bunnykins
Cheeky Boy
Chipie
Cuddlepie
Cutie
Dolly

Doodie
Dotty
Heather
Huggy
Ickey
Koukla
Liebchen
Maisie
Millie
Mr Cheecky
Oocky

Petite Toutou
Pookie
Poppsy
Show Off
Skittles
Snugglepot
Sweetheart
Sweetie Puss
Teddy Bear
Tiddler
Winkie

ELEGANT

Adage
Adeva
Adjani
Aerial
Aleutia
Alicia
Amelia
Anooshka
Arabella
Argenta
Arpege
Beatrice
Bentleigh
Bianca
Bianco
Caniche
Cecilia
Channel
Chintz
Claudette

Clayton
Clicquot
Coco Channel
Constanza
Consuela
Cuthbert
Debonair
Delice
Dolche
Dudley
Edwina
Estelle
Felicity
Gilbert
Grace
Gucci
Jaegar
Marmaduke
Marquise
Martine

Martisse
Maurice
Maxine
Mercedes
Monet
Monique
Montague
Moritz
Musette

Percy
Perrier
Philamena
Philbert
Prudence
Quincy

Raphael
Rhett
Roxanne
Rupert
Seymour
Sir William

Sucher
Tarquin
Tobias
Tobias Horatio
Nelson
Tristram

FAMOUS PEOPLE

Andretti
Attila
Bart
Beans
Biggles
Bing
Bismark
Blake
Blitzen
Bronte
Byron
Campo
Cantona
Carlos
Carlos Felipe
Chomsky
Chopin
Churchill
Clint
Clinton
Columbus
Cosby
Curtly
Di
Dianna
Dillon
Einstein
Elvis

Emily Bronte
Ertha
Farrah
Fergie
Franklin
Grimaldi
Halley
Houdini
Huxley
Jamie Lee
Jango
Julio
Kazamir
Keats
Keiffer
Kippling
Kitchener
Mark Twain
Marlow
Melba
Mingus
Monte
Montgomery
Mozart
Napoleon
Newton
Nijinski
Nikita

Otis
Pavarotti
Picasso
Pushkin
Ravel
Reuben
Ringo
Rommel
Rosencrantz
Satchmo
Schubert
Shackera
Shaq
Sherman
Sibalius
Sigmund
  Freud
Spencer
Strauss
Tolstoy
Twiggy
Tyson
Valentino
Whitney
Whoopie
Yoko
Zola
Zsa Zsa

FOOD & DRINK

Baci
Biscuit
Bollinger
Bolly
Bon Bon
Brandy
Brioche
Brodie
Cappuccino
Casserole
Chablis
Champers
Cherry
Choco
Chocolate
Chocolate
  Cake
Chutney
Cider
Cinnamon
Coca Cola
Coconut
Cognac
Cointreau
Coke
Cola

Croissant
Crumble
Crumbs
Crumpet
Crusty
Custard
Donut
Frascati
Gilbey
Gnocci
Guinness
Jack Daniels
Jaffa
Jim Beam
Kahlua
Kus Kus
Lapsang
Latte
Liquorice
Mango
Marmalade
Marmite
Marzipan
Mintie
Muffin
Noisette

Noodle
Noodles
Pimms
Popcorn
Porridge
Pretzel
Pumpkin
Rum
Safron
Sage
Salt & Pepper
Sambucca
Sausage
Shampers
Shandy
Sherbert
Sherry
Snitzel
Soda
Spinach
Stoli
Strudel
Tangerine
Tequila
Toffee
Vegemite

HI TECH

C D
Macro
Pixel
Quark
Radar

Rocket
Sky Rocket
Sonic
Space Cat
Turbo

HISTORIC

Allethea
Aloysius
Apollo
Argus
Athena
Atticus
Attila
Augustus
Bacchus
Boadicea
Brutus
Caesar
Cassandra
Cassiopaia
Cassius
Cerberus
Chauncey
Cherub
Claudius
Cleopatra
Cupid
Cybil

Cyrus
Czar
Daphne
Dartagnan
Diana
Electra
Eros
Fabian
Figaro
Gilda
Hannibal
Hercules
Hermes
Hero
Homer
Horace
Horatio
Isis
Jason
Julius
Juno
Macina

Mephisto
Nefertiti
Nero
Ophelia
Orpheus
Pendragon
Penelope
Persephone
Pharoah
Plato
Pluto
Rameses
Romulus
Scarob
Socrates
Spartacus
Sybil
Titan
Titus
Tutan
Xena
Xerxes

MAKES ME LAUGH!

Absent
  Minded
Adolph
Aggie
Ampy
Arfer
Assasin
Astro Boy
Bagel

Baggins
Baggy
Batcat
Beast
Beefer
Benoir
Berzacle
Biff
Biffy

Big Doodie
Bimbo
Blast
Blitz
Bozo
Brillow
Bruto
Bugeyes
Buzzy

Bwana
Cactus
Cecil
Cedric
Chungfu
Clousseau
Combat
Commando
Crazy Joe
Critter
Diddle - King
Dizzy
Eccles
Fang
Fat Cat
Fatso
Fuzzy
Gibbitty
Gogo
Goldie Ponx
Gordon
  Bennet
Grub

Gumby
Gummi
Haywire
Itchy
Itchy Boy
Jet Cat
Kali Motxo
Kama (Kazie)
Killa
Knuckle
Lil Pudd
Little Doodie
Mavis
Mayhem
Mildred
Mincer
Monkey
Monster
Mr Biggles
Mr Mush
Mr Stripy
  Pants
Mr Universe

Nappy
Nitro
Noddy
Pesty
Raticuss
Scardy
Scratchy
Shona Mercy
Smiggin
Snapper
Snookums
Splotch
Squadgy
Sumo
The Butler
Tiddly Pom
Toxo
Tweetie Pie
Whiffy
Wickerty Wack
Zonk
Zoomy
Zudnik

NATURE RELATED

Autumn
Bees Wax
Blueberry
Cedar
Cheetah
Chestnut
Cloudy
Clover
Comet
Cotton
Cougar

Crystal
Daffodil
Daisy
Diamond
Emerald
Everest
Flower
Fox
Frangipani
Friday
Fuschia

Goose
Granite
Hawk
Honey
Ice
Jade
Jaguar
Jasmine
Jojoba
Kaos
Leopard

NAME YOUR PET!

Lotus
Luna
Lupus
Moon
Moonbeam
Moose
Mountain Dew
Mushroom
Mustang
Oleander
Olive
Opal
Owl
Panda
Pansy
Pantha
Panther
Pearl
Pearly
Petal
Petunia
Pippin
Pixie
Polar
Pollux
Primrose
Pussy Willow
Rainbow
River
Rocklilly
Rose
Rose Petals
Rosebud
Sapphire
Sequoia
Shamrock
Sirius
Sky
Snow
Snow Beau
Snow Boy
Snowball
Snowdrop
Snowflake
Snowman
Spider
Springtime
Squid
Strawberry
Sunshine
Thunder
Topaz
Velvet
Venus

NEW ZEALANDER

Boozer
Bungy
Chamois
Clarke
Cracker
Ehoa
Geyser
Going
Greenstone
Grub
Haka
Hokey Pokey
Hokonui
Hongi
Jandals
Jonah
Kea
Kino
Kiri
Kiwi
Lady Alice
Manuka
Mockie
Nzer
Orange
Roughy
Otago
Phar Lap
Rutherford
Scott
Smoko
Steinlager
Tapu
Taranaki
Tiki
Toetoe
Wellington
Whineray

ORIGINAL IDEAS

Blackout
Bongo
Boogie
Booker
Boumba
Boyzai
Brat Cat
Bruiser
Bulldozer
Bumper
Bunker
Captain Jack
Catastrophe
Chatter Box
Chubbles
Clawed
Cobweb
Crash
Dimpy
Dodger
Dozer
Dumpster
Feliny
Fidel
Fiver
Foufette

Gaucho
Gertrude
Gingus
Giovanni
Gobelino
Grungle
Gunter
Haggis
Helmut
Honky
Hungry
Jambo
Jarra
Jean Clawed
  Belmondo
Kipper
Kitty Litter
Lickety
Lodger
Lord Angus
Matrix
Mince
Mishy
Mojo
Morse Code
Mr Herriot

Nike
Nippity
Paddles
Paint Tin
Proffessor
Prowler
Purrseus
Queensky
Racer
Ransom
Rasmus
Rory
Rugger
Ruhfus
Slam
Spanner
Speedwell
Spinner
Swampy
Swiggles
T Bone
Tango
Tugger
Tuk Tuk
Waldo
Waxer

PLACE NAMES

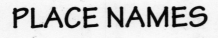

Aberdeen
Alaska
Alberquerque
Alberta
Argyle

Arizona
Aspen
Bega
Brooklyn
Cairo

Calypso
Capri
Casablanca
Chelsea
China

Cleveland
Collingwood
Cosima
Dakota
Dallas
Harlem
Indiana
Irish
Java
Jeddah
Jordan
Kashmir
Kenya

Manly
Melbourne
Montana
Navarro
Odessa
Paddington
Paris
Paris Texas
Pelham
Persia
Pompei
Ponsonby
Rangoon

Rimini
Roman
Seoul
Siam
Sydney
Souchong
Suzuka
Tamil
Texas
Tunguska
Vienna
Windsor
Winnipeg

POP MUSIC

Abba
Bowie
Coolio
Enya
Hendrix

Ice T
Iggy
Ike
Madonna
Mambo

Micah
Rasta
Reggae
Sade
Woodstock

POTENTIALLY CHEEKY

Boner
Butts
Dicko
Doo Doo
Floosie
Floppy
Fozdik
Grotty

Hashish
Kaffa
King Titus
Knickers
Lice
Piddles
Randi
Sarcoma

Scabby
Scuzzie
Sludge
Sluggo
Snurp
Spunky
Strumpet
Tripe

PRETTY

Anastasia
Annabell
Annabella
Anastasia
April
Aurora
Babette
Brigitte
Calico
Celine
Christabel
Collette

Coquette
Daisy
Elka
Fifi
Fleur
Florence
Georgie Girl
Harriette
Imogen
Isabella
Jana
Jessie Belle

Juanita
Liberty
Lucille
Lucinda
Melodie
Merry
Petal
Purdita
Scarlet
Selina
Sweet Pea
Victoria

SUMMARY & NOTES ON YOUR OWN PET'S NAME

SCORE BOARDS

Over the page you will find a few tables so you can easily tabulate your attempts to choose a name. Here are a few ideas on how to get started.

FAMILY DICTATORSHIP

As you browse make a note of 10 names you really like. From these score them out of 10, 1 for your favorite 10 for your least favorite. Reconsider the order of the top three names and there you have it, a well considered name for your pet!

DEMOCRATIC FAMILY VOTE

Have a show of hands on the voting for the 10 names you have chosen. Tally the count (people can vote once for any of the names they like). The highest tally wins. For equal firsts, just draw from a hat. Then, having dragged the family through this be malevolent and just choose one yourself!

I'M HOPELESS AND CANNOT CHOOSE 10 NAMES

Well you are hopeless aren't you? Open the pages randomly 10 times and choose 10 names with your eyes closed, using a pin. Do not carry out this procedure if you have been drinking heavily!

NAME YOUR PET!

	Names You Like	Your Score	Democratic Vote Tally
1			
2			
3			
4			
5			
6			
7			
8			
9			
10			

	Names You Like	Your Score	Democratic Vote Tally
1			
2			
3			
4			
5			
6			
7			
8			
9			
10			